HIDDEN GARDENS
OF THE
CHANNEL ISLANDS

JERSEY

HIDDEN GARDENS
OF THE
CHANNEL ISLANDS

TEXT
Lynne Jenner

PHOTOGRAPHY
Lynne Jenner • Gary Grimshaw

ILLUSTRATIONS
Nigel Jenner

AUTHOR'S ACKNOWLEDGEMENTS

Thanks are due to the owners and gardeners who have shared their intimate
knowledge with me, have allowed me to turn up at odd and sometimes
inconvenient times and who have rummaged through files to find particulars
or an odd plant name. Thanks also to the many friends and family who have
supported me over the years and who have encouraged me to continue when I
have felt despondent, particularly to my husband, Nigel who is always there
when I need him and who has tirelessly produced such wonderful illustrations.
Lastly a special thankyou to Barbara and the late Roy Overland who have
sponsored the photography, to John Best who has sponsored the scanning and
to Marcus Binney who kindly agreed to write the foreword.

Hamamelis x *intermedia* 'Jelena'

First published in Great Britain in 2002
by Capensis Publishing Ltd
PO Box 260, 4 & 6 Broad Street
St Helier, Jersey JE4 8TS

ISBN 0 - 9542386 - 0 - 5

Designer Anthony Aspland Associates
Printed by Butler & Tanner

CONTENTS

To Nigel with all my love

Jersey is a paradise for gardeners. A mild climate and fertile soil make it possible to grow an astonishing range of trees, shrubs and flowers. Part of the thrill of gardening in Jersey is the sheer speed at which plants grow, faster by far than many parts of the mainland. Jersey also offers a range of micro-climates - almost subtropical by the sea on the south coast, sheltered south-facing sites basking in sun from morning to evening on the heights above St. Aubin's Bay, protected valleys inland, slopes running down to sheltered coves on the north coast and sandy soils behind the beautiful bays of St. Brelade and St. Ouen.

A Frenchman who came to Jersey at the end of the Napoleonic wars described it as a kingdom of Lilliput, composed of little hills and little streams. Gardeners in Jersey have taken advantage of this topography and there are gardens which have descended valleys and colonised slopes, which have grown round protected ponds or been bravely staked out on windy heights protected by new planting.

As every visitor to this island discovers, many of the delights of Jersey architecture are tucked away down country lanes. The gardens are often even more hidden away so this book will bring revelations and delights to everyone who looks at it.

FOREWORD

Marcus Binney OBE February 13, 2002

IN HARMONY WITH NATURE

Hidden away down a long leafy track is 'Judith's Garden' at 'Creux
Baillot Cottage'. Visually stunning, every inch is crammed with flowers
to give scent and colour throughout the spring and summer. It is also
an ecological paradise. Increasing numbers of birds take refuge
including woodpeckers. Self-sown fennel attracts hoverflies, buddlejas
are fodder for Red Admiral butterflies and berries and seedheads are
left to nurture and encourage wildlife.

above: *A boardwalk allows a closer inspection of moisture-loving perennials.*

over far left: *A shimmering dragonfly clings onto gently swaying flower spikes of* Stipa tenuissima.

middle: *Half hardy salvias mingle with* Agastache foeniculum *and* Tricyrtis formosana 'Shelley's' *in a haze of blue and mauve.*

top: *Perennials jostle for space and prevent emerging weeds.*

bottom: *A shaft of sunlight on a shady corner where* Pulmonaria 'Majeste' *enjoys the conditions.*

To listen to self-taught plantswoman Judith Querée is inspiring as her enthusiasm is hard to restrain. With fifteen hundred perennials in her three quarter acre plot it is amazing that she can recall not just their Latin names but their country of origin and symbolic associations. Working as a team, Judith's husband Nigel is equally at home in the garden and tackles all the hard landscaping, boardwalks, paths and numerous plant supports.

It was twenty five years ago when they unexpectedly discovered the cottage, derelict, amongst a deluge of old bedsteads, rusting cars and beer bottles. Once the rubbish had been cleared the soil was sieved and compost added before planting could begin. Hard to believe now, as Judith says "I have to pinch myself sometimes to be sure it is all real".

Little vignettes catch your eye wherever you turn, a colourful windmill, the silvery-ribbed foliage of celmisia in pots amongst driftwood, pebbles and shells, a copper dragonfly and perennials galore. A striking plant *Mertensia simplicissima* with incredibly glaucous foliage sits at the base of *Billardiera longiflora* and *Clematis rehderiana* and around the corner, facing south, blue flowered *Sollya heterophylla* hugs a late flowering *Clematis crispa*.

In the borders can be found all sorts of treasures; half hardy salvias, including carmine *Salvia involucrata* and the clear blue *S. uliginosa* and *S. patens* 'Cambridge Blue', *Clematis* x *aromatica* and *Clematis* 'Arabella' spiralling around supports crafted by Nigel and a late summer group of *Strobilanthes atropurpurea*,

Agastache foeniculum and *Tricyrtis formosana* 'Shelley's'. Colours are muted – hazy mauves and purples with just the odd splash of bright yellow or orange to sharpen the senses. Often asked about how to prune clematis, Judith who now has over one hundred varieties, maintains that if they flower before the longest day they should be cut hard to the ground after flowering.

As more land is acquired from the neighbouring farmer, so Judith is able to indulge her passion. A path behind the greenhouse, meanders through dense planting on a sloping

bank down to a recently constructed boardwalk where you can look down onto a woven tapestry of moisture-lovers. *Aconitum paniculatum*, *Gladiolus papilio,* panicum and alliums give way to lythrum, rudbeckias, lobelias including the luscious *Lobelia* 'Dark Crusader' and linarias. *Rosa* 'Francis E. Lester' clambers through an old tree while tucked into its bole is *Rosa* x *odorata* 'Mutabilis'. Old tree trunks are left in situ and ferns revel in the shady conditions.

This is a garden to walk around and delight in. Returning up towards the house, just before a wonderful late flowering *Clematis* x *triternata*, is the secret of every gardener's success. The compost, a lasagne of horse manure, woody material, thin layers of grass clippings, seaweed, kitchen waste and newspaper.

In autumn the garden is cut down to the ground and put to rest for the winter until early in February, the first snowdrops stir from dormancy and it all springs to life again.

top: Rudbeckia fulgida *var.* deamii *makes a dazzling picture with red and blue lobelias.*

above: *Lichen and fallen tree trunks are left to encourage wildlife.*

A GOLD AND SILVER ARENA

Marcus and Anne Binney inherited 'Domaine des Vaux' and its five acre garden, about fifteen years ago from Lady Binney, Marcus's mother. Lady Binney belonged to that generation of inspired gardeners who had both the time, enthusiasm, and horticultural knowledge to mastermind and implement gardens on a grand scale.

Marcus's parents moved to Jersey in 1969 exchanging the heavy clay of their large Elizabethan house, 'Horham Hall' in Essex for a pink granite farmhouse that nestled into the hillside and was at that time surrounded completely by arable fields.

Influenced by a love of Italian gardens and excited by the prospect of gardening on the lighter and more hospitable soil of Jersey, Sir George and Lady Binney enlisted the help of architect Walter Ison and together, after major earth moving, fashioned the surrounding land into a formal Italianate arena.

right: *Beyond an Italianate well-head, the tiered borders overflow with colourful and aromatic shrubs. A weeping pear,* Pyrus salicifolia *'Pendula' dominates the silver and grey bed.*

facing page: *Shafts of sunlight add an air of mystery and intrigue to the statue of Apollo and Daphne which is almost hidden under a bower of honeysuckle and* Clematis montana.

With an artistic eye and a wonderful sense of colour, Lady Binney skilfully composed one side in silver and grey and the facing side in yellow, gold and bronze. The tiered borders now overflow with colourful and aromatic shrubs. Pineapple-scented Moroccan broom, *Cytisus battandieri*, honey-scented daisy bushes, furry ballota, sea buckthorn, artemisia, caryopteris and shrubby willows. Wrapping around the end of the arena a large *Pyrus salicifolia* 'Pendula' acts as a foil to the predominately purple and pink colour scheme.

Next to another honey-scented shrub, *Pittosporum tenuifolium* 'Purpureum' is a mushroom-shaped *Acer palmatum* 'Dissectum Atropurpureum' and a large *Magnolia* x *soulangeana*. With careful

granny's bonnets. Echiums tower above other perennials and seed themselves liberally and a surprise gourd flourishes amongst the lavender!

Almost hidden beneath a bower of honeysuckle and *Clematis montana* is a good copy of Bernini's statue of Apollo and Daphne. Greek mythology tells us of Apollo's love for Daphne and her transformation into a laurel tree on fearing his advances.

Standing in the Rose Garden one can admire the superb views over the arena and down to the semi-wild garden that falls away steeply to the valley below. A singularly beautiful sight in late February is a *Magnolia campbellii*; that twenty eight years later,

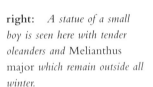

right: *A statue of a small boy is seen here with tender oleanders and* Melianthus major *which remain outside all winter.*

far right: *A shady corner in which to sit under the canopy of a honey locust,* Gleditsia triacanthos *and* Myrtus luma. *Lady's mantle self-sows abundantly into cracks between the paving.*

colour transition the borders then acquire gold and bronze hues shot with touches of dark red. *Lonicera nitida* 'Baggessen's Gold' intermixed with ligularias; *Elaeagnus pungens* 'Maculata' and *Euonymus fortunei* 'Emerald 'n' Gold' with euphorbias and hostas.

A garden never stands still and as with most designs, scale must always be kept in check. Dark sentinel-like cypress trees originally planted to give a strong architectural framework have been removed having outgrown their allotted space. The White Garden can now be seen to advantage. Metal hoops festooned with white 'Iceberg' roses and everlasting sweetpeas are underplanted with white flowering plants; hesperis, valerian and

truly encapsulates the spirit of Lady Binney's accomplished planting. A garden reflects the character and personality of its owners and it is fortunate that both Marcus and Anne are as passionate now about the conservation and future of the garden. Every year in July, the Italianate arena becomes a stage set for three unforgettable nights of opera in a setting that is as theatrical as it is romantic.

In summer, the sheltered terrace is host to a profusion of sun-loving and tender varieties. Choice climbers dress the house walls; a climbing geranium, a potato vine, *Solanum jasminoides* 'Album' and a Chinese gooseberry, *Actinidia chinensis*. *Melianthus major* makes a handsome partner for white and pink oleanders that remain outside all winter and flower prolifically during a long hot summer. In the centre is a small fountain, a boy on a dolphin blowing his trumpet conch - the effect of its spray soothing on a warm day. Procumbent roses, 'The Fairy' and 'Nozomi' billow out from raised planters and lady's mantle charmingly distributes itself amongst the paving, but the favourite must be a magnificent *Myrtus luma*. In late summer the white flowers are heady with scent and humming with bees and a *Gleditsia triacanthos* provides a wonderful umbrella under which to sit and unwind.

The lower garden is semi-natural. A path leads the visitor by the little Mediterranean Garden and down through semi-circular

orchard terraces - a delight in summer when branches arch dramatically beneath the weight of ripe apples, plums and crab-apples. Past a wide-spreading *Parrotia persica* to a bank of Californian poppies, *Romneya coulteri,* always a talking point when their wide crinkly petals open to look like huge fried eggs.

A string of ponds provide hours of fascination for the Binney's springer spaniels who bound across the water channels into the dense clumps of tall bamboos. Conifers and eucalyptus make a tapestry of green and grey and form a glorious backdrop to a large willow that weeps generously over a *Gunnera manicata,* water iris, arums, bergenias and ferns. Beyond is a natural

above left: *The attractive trunk of a fast-growing eucalyptus adds an almost subtropical effect and, together with other evergreens, forms a tapestry of green and grey in the valley providing a solid backdrop to the waterside planting.*

above: *A lemon tree revels in the warmth of a sheltered terrace.*

woodland which Anne is keen to extend. At its best in Spring when lit by wild narcissi and bluebells, Anne is gradually reducing the number of sycamores and planting alternative native species. Emerging from the shady woodland canopy, a path meanders through a Camellia Walk back to the house.

The Herb and Kitchen Gardens are the result of Anne's inspiration. An awkward corner near the house has been

transformed into a small formal herb garden using green and variegated box which Anne grew from cuttings.

The Kitchen Garden is entered through small white gates flanked by clipped bay trees. Inspired by Rosemary Verey's potager at 'Barnsley House' in Gloucestershire, Anne has cleverly divided it into diamond-shaped beds using box edging and planted it with a mixture of both flowers for cutting and vegetables. It is a productive garden and almost everything is rotated; sweet peas alternate with runner beans that scramble over pliable hoops, an idea that she first saw at 'Highgrove House', the Prince of Wales' garden. Narrow borders may be planted one year with ornamental cabbages and the following year with basil or parsley or maybe even a row of leeks. Each year a plan is drawn up, rotating crops to new positions. Next year Anne is going to try more vegetables and less flowers "I love growing beans – they freeze jolly well", she says with enthusiasm.

17

above: *The kitchen garden provides cut flowers and vegetables for the household and is entered through a small white gate flanked by clipped bay trees*

left: *The beautiful peeling bark of a multi-stem myrtle,* Myrus luma *catches the sunlight making it look all the more startling. In late summer it is a mass of delicate white flowers.*

A GREEN OASIS

In thirty five years Ansell and Rollo Hawkins have successfully established the garden of their dreams.

When they moved to 'Cap Verd House' from New Zealand, in 1966, there was a semblance of a garden. A plastic lined pool near the house, five square rose beds filled with 'Frensham' roses (of which a few still remain), three large *Cupressus macrocarpa* and everywhere straight lines.

Although not extensive in size, by using gentle curves the Hawkins have masterminded an illusion of space using a framework of hardy plants to create a 'room' in the middle of a 'forest'. As you stroll around the garden, and stroll you must because there are so many unusual specimens to see, an atmosphere of calm and tranquility enfolds you.

In front of the house at the base of a vine-clad verandah, a dull conifer has had its skirt raised, resulting in a magnificent sculptured feature and a dome-shaped box has been cleverly topiarised into a seat. Nearby a majestic thirty year old *Quercus robur* 'Fastigiata' (which the Hawkins first saw in Russia where they are used as street trees) is planted next to a large bay, *Laurus nobilis* 'Aurea', which is particularly striking in winter when the leaves turn to a rich buttery gold.

The skilful juxtaposition of shapes can be seen, at first contrasting and then merging into a harmonious picture, as the planting gently wraps around the whole length and breadth of the garden. Interesting trees include *Gleditsia triacanthos* 'Elegantissima' with fern-like leaves and a rare medium-sized tree *Tilia henryana* with soft downy foliage, a black mulberry, a tulip tree, and a *Cryptomeria japonica* 'Spiralis' with leaves that coil around its branches, sometimes called 'Grannie's Ringlets.'

Major Hawkins is particularly delighted with a specimen *Nyssa sinensis* which not only has young red growth but also has the most marvellous fiery autumn tints regardless of the weather and appears to be more reliable for a stunning display than the more commonly planted *Nyssa sylvatica*.

In the corner, an old storm damaged oak acts as a host to an evergreen creeper, *Hydrangea integerrima,* from Chile which has wound its way up to a height of six metres or more. Flowers similar to white shaving brushes give an intriguing display in late summer and follow on from the showy inflorescences of a *Hydrangea sargentiana*.

Various sitting areas have been created to give dappled shade at various times of the day. Around the sunken terrace at the far end of the garden, trees were planted to create a sense of enclosure. The *Pinus wallichiana* trunks have visibly swelled and a Mount Etna broom has grown to over ten metres in height, each year producing a mass of yellow blooms in July.

A delightful granite seat (part of an old apple crusher), tucked into a corner overlooking a small raised lily pond, is surrounded by lush planting in front of a backdrop of laurel. Here perennials and grasses mingle naturally, shimmering silver foliage and aromatics effectively acting as a foil to the brighter golden grasses. Throughout the garden there is a noticeable repetition of favourite perennials but used with different effects.

over: *Old tree trunks have become useful seats and nestle into a delicious mix of grasses, perennials and contrasting foliage.*

below left: *At the base of a vine-clad verandah, a dull conifer has had its skirt raised, resulting in a strong sculptural effect.*

below: *An elegant statue is framed by a Gleditsia triacanthos 'Sunburst' which is particularly striking when shafts of early evening sunlight gleam through the tracery of finely cut leaves. Seen here with the fiery young leaves of* Photinia x fraseri *'Red Robin' and* Geranium maderense.

right: *Silhouetted in a cool shady corner, an unusual sculpture becomes an interesting focal point highlighted by the fresh fronds of hardy ferns.*

A little further on, dominating the scene, a deep gold *Chamaecyparis lawsoniana* 'Winston Churchill' planted in 1968 adds substance to an elegant *Gleditsia triacanthos* 'Sunburst' which is particularly striking when shafts of early evening sunlight gleam through its tracery of finely cut leaves. An *Eriobotrya japonica* contrasts boldly with heavily ribbed leathery leaves and a female *Podocarpus salignus* from Chile conceals small berries tucked beneath masses of evergreen willow-like leaves. (The male is hidden around the corner!).

top far right: *Each of the seating areas has its own distinctive character. Here, insulated from the outside world, Chinese gooseberries,* Actinidia chinensis *provide a wealth of heart-shaped leaves that scramble over a pergola and if favoured with a hot summer, will also provide a good crop of fruit.*

middle far right: *A fine specimen* Gleditsia triacanthos *'Sunburst' with bright golden leaves draws the eye towards the furthest end of the garden. Seen here against darker evergreens that provide a contrast of both shape and texture.*

bottom far right: *A granite trough becomes a natural setting for shade-loving ferns and ivies.*

In the shade cast by two *Magnolia sprengeri* and backed by the peeling tawny-coloured bark of a *Myrtus luma* is a delightful enclosed terrace where time is of no consequence. Old tree trunks have become useful seats and nestle into a delicious mix of contrasting foliage, *Libertia formosa*, grasses, daylilies, violas, aromatic marjorams, rue, fennel and a lovely *Stipa gigantea* which retains its deep gold flower stems all summer. A rare x *Sycoparrotia*

semidecidua, a cross between a parrotia and a sycopsis, enjoys the protection of a wall. But the most remarked on tree in the garden is a *Sophora japonica* 'Pendula' with its tortuous interior growth.

A Chinese yew, *Taxus celebica,* with lush yellowish-green leaves conceals the small vegetable garden. Bordering the path the tender *Geranium maderense* adds a carefree charm to the many sedge grasses which were originally sown from seed brought back from New Zealand, including the bronze coloured *Carex buchananii.*

The top of the valley with its natural stream was acquired some years after the house and has since been planted with trees. Quinces that fruit prolifically conceal the thousand gallon water tanks (a necessity in times of drought) and seven different cultivars of filbert, *Corylus maxima* ensure maximum production of cobnuts which are shared equally between the Hawkins and the red squirrels. The Turkish hazel, *Corylus colurna,* has interesting corky corrugations on its bark but does not produce any nuts. Other more stately trees include the silver lime, *Tilia tomentosa,* the beautiful Japanese white birch, *Betula platyphylla japonica* and a rare *Nyssa aquatica* which is now classed as a Champion tree and has reached over four metres in height and eight metres in diameter. A fine specimen of *Maackia amurensis* flowers throughout July and early August, and benefiting from the moisture near the stream are a *Metasequoia glyptostroboides* and contorted willow, *Salix matsudana* 'Tortuosa'. In spring a most unusual willow, *Salix magnifica* produces catkins at the same time as large magnolia-like leaves.

Ansell and Rollo have created a garden for all seasons; a luxuriant green oasis which becomes fully furnished in summer and in which colour plays a subtle role.

right: *A colourful portrait with marsh marigolds,* Caltha palustris. *A menagerie of animals is likely to greet you on arrival.*

A CORNER OF PARADISE

Passing a wonderful 95 year old handkerchief tree, *Davidia involucrata,* and leaving behind a picturesque wooded valley just a stroll from the sea is a small unobtrusive entrance concealing a paradise garden rising up to a pinnacle 200 feet above sea level where a pavilion offers some respite and a magnificent view.

To meet Rhona, Lady Guthrie for the first time is a memorable experience. Her enthusiasm and wit evoke a sparkle that can be glimpsed as you walk around her garden. Note the little muslin bags filled with persuasive offerings hanging on a *Sophora tetraptera* to lure the blue tits away from the hanging clusters of yellow flower buds and the charming whimsical details such as the wild geese sculptures that greet you on arrival and the menagerie of animals that she is so fond of congregating in the courtyard. Peacocks strut on the garage roof, cockateels fly around the garden room and red squirrels scamper amongst the trees.

Thirty five years ago when Sir Giles and Lady Guthrie acquired the house 'Les Vaux' (built around 1840), it had become sadly neglected, but it had a certain charm and the pink granite farmhouse and small barn to the rear were pretty. It took about two years to clear the Christmas tree plantation, bramble, bracken and pernicious weeds before Lady Guthrie could consider planting and only a North American swamp cypress and a purple beech have been retained from the original scheme. Over the years more land has been acquired and now there are in excess of three acres in cultivation.

It is not the easiest garden to work or maintain as the cliff face rises sharply either side of the wide path. Photographs tend to flatten the image, but from the top the sheer drop can be clearly seen. Visitors think that the garden is very sheltered but the south facing *côtil* has similarities to the Gobi desert and the north-east face receives only early morning sun. Plants have been carefully chosen to adapt to such diverse requirements.

An inspirational idea, which Lady Guthrie admits is not totally original, are the swags of woven ivy that decorate the granite wall at the side of the house. Now that it has thickened sufficiently all that is needed is an occasional trim. On the bank above, the young foliage of a Golden rain tree,

Koelreuteria paniculata, glows in warm shrimp pink tones against a clear blue sky and contrasts with the new growth of *Photinia* x *fraseri* 'Red Robin'

From a muddy pool and natural stream, small waterfalls were created to give constant water throughout the year although they do

top far left: *The côtil can be seen rising steeply behind this statue of a boy.*

middle far left: *An intimate corner. Note the granite trough balanced on heavy stone weights.*

bottom far left: *Ivy swags add elegance to a granite wall and need only an occasional clipping to maintain their shape. Beyond can be seen the pavilion which offers spectacular views back down to the house and garden.*

above left: *Paths traverse the steep hillsides and allow access to the rhododendrons, azaleas and pieris that create such a colourful scene each spring.*

above: *The spears of New Zealand flax,* Phormium tenax *contrast dramatically with the smooth volcanic rock (or pudding stone as it is known locally) echoed in the foreground by the vertical leaves of a white flowering* Iris ensata.

sometimes dry out in a hot summer. The late Mr. Reginald Perry, of Perry's Hardy Plant Farm gave advice for the original waterside planting. A contorted willow, *Salix babylonica* var. *pekinensis* 'Tortuosa' rises above impressive groups of Solomon's seal, caltha, primulas and hostas together with *Iris ensata, Zantedeschia aethiopica* and daylily cultivars. A favourite shrub is the divine prostrate willow, *Salix fruticulosa,* whose creeping stems produce brownish-pink catkins early in the year.

In spring a spectacular splash of vibrant, exploding colour stops you in your tracks, crimson, magenta and shocking pink sharply contrasting with the volcanic rock (or pudding stone as it is known locally). These evergreen azaleas were enthusiastically planted into the deep crevices that had become exposed after Lady Guthrie and her gardener had together removed a stand of mature sycamores by rigging up a block and tackle. More recently, Lady Guthrie has tempered their ferocious colours by adding some white into the stunning display. Sorbus add to their deeper hues in the autumn.

At the western end the remains of an orchard was cleared and the earth was pushed back and raised to form a platform. To create interest a pavilion acts as a focal point and offers dramatic views back down to the house and garden. At one time wild broom covered the rock face, and was enjoyed for a number of years until it eventually became too leggy. It was removed and instead the whole area was planted with species that will survive the dry conditions including rock roses and phlomis. *Rosmarinus officinalis* 'Prostratus' which although quite tender (a severe winter will wipe out the entire plantation which is now approximately thirty metres across) is a spectacle in the spring when it is smothered with bright blue flowers.

The introduction of *Hypericum calycinum* was felt to be a frightful error as it developed rust and its invasive qualities smothered other treasures and new plantings such as a favourite conifer, *Cunninghamia lanceolata*. *Grevillea rosmarinifolia* flowers profusely enjoying the well drained

conditions, and a *Drimys winteri* provides fragrant ivory flowers in late April and May. *Rosa* 'Grouse' has proved to be a success covering three metres each season, pegged down at regular intervals to keep it low and spreading and the half hardy little *Polygonum capitatum* is an enchantress covering the rock face with tiny pink flowers throughout the summer, although it does die back in winter. Further along *Acacia melanoxylon* are beginning to colonise the steep banks.

A few years ago over thirty thousand bulbs from Holland were planted, mainly daffodils and blue *Anemone blanda* which give a glorious spring show. Lady Guthrie recalls that Joe the gardener gathered together some of his friends and, using a wonderful tool that you can only find in Madeira, three men managed to plant fifteen thousand bulbs in three days.

A plant hunter and great friend, Tony Schilling, suggested to Lady Guthrie that she should have more winter interest and so yellow stemmed willows, *Salix alba* var. *vitellina,* were planted, together with various dogwoods including the red stemmed *Cornus alba* 'Sibirica' and the purple stemmed variety that are so dark that they look practically black. A magnificent *Betula utilis* has almost outgrown its position, but it is such a joy in the winter when the white skeleton can be seen from the bedroom window. The trunk is scrubbed each year to retain its white bark.

A grove of Himalayan birch and three types of alder have been planted on the more recently acquired hillside above the entrance which was previously cultivated with potatoes. "My first idea when I got this *côtil* was to make it wild, so at enormous expense I bought pounds and pounds of wild flower seeds. It was a great business sowing them. Now, not one but five years later, I counted six precious cowslips which gave me more excitement than if you had presented me with the rarest of orchids, so now I inspect in case some other surprise awaits me".

Below is a tender bead tree, *Melia azedarach*, grown from seed that was collected on one of Lady Guthrie's trips to Greece. Now recorded as a Champion of Great Britain it thrives facing east and without protection, except from the hill behind, and every year without fail produces fragrant star-shaped flowers during the summer which can best be seen from the higher paths.

The sweet scent of *Pittosporum tobira* can be detected beside the narrow path leading down to the lower garden, and the lilac foxglove flowers of a *Paulownia tomentosa* can be glimpsed through the trees. Beyond, Mexican orange blossom, *Choisya ternata*, fills a difficult spot and together with the pure white 'Casa Blanca' lilies creates a deliciously scented corner prior to a Mount Etna broom, *Genista aetnensis*, becoming the star attraction.

Walking up the gently sloping lawn towards the house is a wonderfully shaped *Albizia julibrissin* 'Rosea' again grown from seed collected on one of Lady Guthrie's travels. This graceful, spreading tree flowers in late summer when it becomes a mass of pink powder puffs. At the lower level are extensive plantings of perennials and grasses including *Ophiopogon planiscapus* 'Nigrescens' and *Molinia caerulea*.

Across the drive is a pygmy pinetum originally planned by Adrian Bloom and planted with about two thousand plants. Although these have gradually been thinned, Lady Guthrie is happy to trim the conifers as necessary where they have overgrown into and around each other to maintain their dramatic effect. Steps flanked by two Doric columns lead back to the courtyard.

Lady Guthrie's energy remains undiminished as she continues to add new features. Following her severe flirtation as she describes it, with the Malus family, when many new trees were added, her latest venture has been to turn a damp meadow into a wild nature reserve by creating two ponds and planting around one hundred native trees including young oak, sweet chestnut, ash and hazel. This is no mean feat at the age of eighty two years with only one gardener. But then Lady Gutherie is a plantswoman who always rises to a challenge.

above: *High above the house and the pair of Doric columns, primroses naturalise on the banks.*

A GARDEN FOR ALL YEAR

Surprisingly close to the town centre, the one and a quarter acre garden at 'Little Croft' is a peaceful haven. The only sounds to be heard are a trickling fountain and the invisible and yet audible sound of church bells ringing.

The area around the house (built in 1933) was originally laid out as a market garden with hedges planted in straight lines and over one hundred apple trees. In 1964 Donald and Jane Sayers purchased the property and have gradually removed all the old fruit trees. Dr. Sayers remembers shuddering at the amount of work that needed doing, but with patience and perseverance, the garden has evolved into what you see today. Now there is an atmosphere of relaxed informality and intimacy provided by the curving borders and narrow winding paths.

29

above: *There is a strong emphasis on plant structure and a bold use of evergreen trees and shrubs.*

The conservatory, a later addition, looks out onto a spacious open lawn, which is framed by tall trees, the verticality giving an illusion of infinity. Dominating a corner near the house, a magnificent multi-stemmed *Liriodendron tulipifera* is a spectacle in June and early July when its spreading branches are lit with distinctive yellow-green tulip-shaped flowers.

There is particular emphasis on plant architecture and the many evergreen trees and shrubs provide interest all year round with their tonal foliage and bold structural forms. For this reason alone, conifers play an important role in the winter scene.

Passing between a weeping willow and a birch a well established blue Atlas cedar, *Cedrus atlantica* Glauca Group is encircled with an underplanting of shimmering *Festuca glauca*. Close by is another cedar, *Cedrus deodara* 'Aurea' and a liquidamber and variegated maple, *Acer platanoides* 'Drummondii' lighten the scene in early summer. Sedges such as *Carex morrowii* and *Carex buchananii* edge a linear border of fuschias and, at the far end of the long lawn are rhododendrons and azaleas which flourish in the acid soil. A striking combination is a purple beech that contrasts with a weeping silver pear, *Pyrus salicifolia* 'Pendula' and the graceful Nootka cypress, *Chamaecyparis nootkatensis* 'Pendula'. All around are subtle cameos of contrasting form, colour and texture, occasionally shot with sudden splashes of vibrant colour such as the bright red 'Frensham' roses amongst green ferns and arum lilies and the scarlet begonias tucked into odd corners.

Near a row of Lane's golden cypresses which conceal 'The Engine Room' of the garden (the compost bins) is a heather bed. Here conifers mingle with heathers and ferns, *Thujopsis dolobrata* and the prostrate *Juniperus communis* 'Repanda' and a group of five tall Irish junipers, *Juniperus communis* 'Hibernica' jokingly known as 'the hen and chickens'; the taller planted over thirty years ago presiding over the 'chickens' which were planted two decades later.

A group of three *Betula utilis* var. *jacquemontii* make an outstanding feature in winter silhouetted against the sombre evergreens whilst in summer *Clematis* x *jackmanii* clambers high into their branches. A low hedge of *Pleioblastus auricomus* returns along the meandering path back to the house - a shady walk where bamboos, camellias and a fine *Pieris formosa* var. *forrestii* enjoy the cool conditions and hostas, bergenias and ferns including *Dryopteris erythrosora* and the exquisite Japanese painted fern, *Athyrium niponicum pictum* colonise the ground.

top: *A clematis and* Acer platanoides *'Drummondii' showing a wonderful contrast between the velvety purple clematis petals and the pale yellow variegated foilage.*

bottom: *A group of five tall Irish junipers,* Juniperus communis *'Hibernica' are jokingly known as 'the hen and chickens'.*

By contrast through an arch smothered in 'Cerise Bouquet' roses, which have a very long flowering season, is another smaller enclosure and another change of mood, backed by a tall hedge of the fragrant *Thuja plicata* 'Atrovirens'. Here eucalyptus and hebes together with an Australian wattle revel in the warmth and shelter alongside the small vegetable area which supplies the household with all its requirements.

A granite apple crusher is the centrepiece of the south lawn, planted with sun-loving species such as diascias, rock roses and stonecrops. Hydrangeas and camellias line the far bed and planted in the lawn are a specimen Sawara cypress, *Chamaecyparis pisifera* 'Squarrosa Sulphurea' and a Spanish blue fir, *Abies pinsapo* 'Glauca'. A new acquisition is an unusual Norfolk Island pine, *Araucaria heterophylla* which is a close relative of the monkey puzzle tree.

Creating a brilliant splash of colour near the tennis court is a wonderful summer grouping of *Hydrangea macrophylla* 'Westfalen', purple berberis, fuschia and a purple flowered clematis romping into the golden-yellow leaves of a *Robinia pseudoacacia* 'Frisia'. Climbing roses surround the court itself adding their perfume on a summer evening.

For Dr Sayers, winter is the busiest time of the year. The Sayers take a critical look and maintain a fairly ruthless policy "The garden isn't a nursing home for plants and if they are not fulfilling their place then I am afraid they have to go. It is a general excuse-me in winter" says Dr Sayers "plants get moved around and hopefully things have improved over the years".

left: *The peeling bark of* Acer griseum *catches the setting sun.*

below: *An apple crusher is planted with a profusion of sun-loving alpines including pink* Diascia vigilis.

A
CLASSIC DOMAIN

Surrounding an elegant Palladian style house 'La Maison des Pres' is a two acre garden that has gradually developed over the last seventeen years under the watchful eye of Lord and Lady Brownlow. A keen gardener, Shirley, Lady Brownlow vividly recalls their first year and the feeling of devastation when bitterly cold winds resulted in severe losses of their young plants.
Plants were replaced, but only once a sufficient framework of evergreen shrubs had been established with the assistance of permanent wind-break material.

Of note on the drive are a tulip tree, *Liriodendron tulipifera* now sixteen years old and a striking evergreen shrub, *Viburnum odoratissimum* whose fragrant white flowers are carried in large conical panicles during late summer.

above: *Box and topiary form an impressive sight from the windows, particularly in winter. The quaint white seat makes a charming addition and adds a touch of informality.*

Huge square tubs containing holm oaks, *Quercus ilex* stand
sentinel either side of the front door, successfully withstanding
the wind that whistles across the forecourt. From here you can
see down to a small pond that is thickly planted with marginals,
and broad leaf species such as *Rheum palmatum, Darmera peltata,
Hosta sieboldiana* var. *elegans, Zantedeschia aethiopica* 'Crowborough'
and the more unusual *Z.a.* 'Green Goddess' which has green and
white spathes.

Notable trees and shrubs near the pond include *Drimys winteri*, a
Betula utilis var. *jacquemontii*, one of the most attractive birches
with striking white bark, *Hydrangea arborescens* 'Annabelle' with
conspicuous rounded heads of creamy white flowers that
continue into early autumn and *Grevillea rosmarinifolia* which in
mild summers produces deep crimson flowers.

top left: *The parterre in
summer. Pink mophead hydrangeas
frame an archway through the yew
hedge. In the foreground is a pot of
Echeveria elegans.*

top right: *One of several
terracotta pots filled with
Echeveria elegans.*

bottom left: *A high wall offers
protection to climbers and creepers
including* Solanum rantonnetii
and plants such as catmint and
Perovskia atriplicifolia *'Blue
Spire' spill over onto the gravel
path, breaking the edge and
creating a sense of movement. On
the right can be seen a smoke tree,
with large panicles of flowers that
look from a distance, like puffs of
pink smoke.*

bottom right: *The fleshy red
and white petals of a pineapple
guava,* Acca sellowiana *are edible
and taste delicious with ice cream.*

33

Through a honeysuckle arch at the side of the house, a shady corner is cleverly planted with yellow flowered shrubs and gold foliage, adding a sunny touch amongst the dark greens. A Mount Etna broom, *Genista aetnensis* overhangs *Phlomis fruticosa* and a golden privet, *Ligustrum ovalifolium* 'Aureum', a shrub that is so often under appreciated. Beyond is the Wild Garden where plants are allowed to

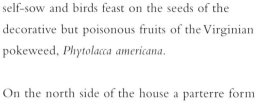

self-sow and birds feast on the seeds of the decorative but poisonous fruits of the Virginian pokeweed, *Phytolacca americana*.

On the north side of the house a parterre forms an impressive sight from the windows particularly on a grey winter's day. The neat geometry, a pattern of four squares surrounding a central rectangle outlined in dwarf box, *Buxus sempervirens* is backed by the tight dark foliage of yew. Variegated hollies, clipped at the end of the summer, punctuate the corners and elegant glazed pots are filled with the grey rosettes and long lasting flowers of *Echeveria elegans.*

Throughout the seasons scented shrubs fill the borders near the parterre; *Daphne laureola, Pittosporum tenuifolium, Olearia* x *haastii, Osmanthus armatus* and for evening fragrance, the potent *Cestrum parqui.*

There is usually something here in flower, whatever the time of year-Lady Brownlow's eyes wander as she notices a favourite plant (Leptospermum) "Quite extraordinary, I thought that I had lost them, and they have seeded themselves! I am crazy for blue and absolutely adore these", pointing to a little group of *Oxypetalum caeruleum* which she grew from seed. Pale green flowered tobacco plants fill any gaps. Seed is obtained either from Chiltern Seeds or Plant World Botanic Gardens. "Chiltern I go to because the catalogue makes such wonderful bedtime reading!"

Through an opening in the yew hedge, made just wide enough to carry a tray through, is a large spreading chestnut and across from the lawn is a semi-circular summer house. Entry to the Secret Garden with its clipped bay trees and divided beds, is most rewarding if approached this way, pausing briefly to admire the heavy crop of muscat grapes and the kneeling figure of an archer; one of three unusual replicas of the celebrated terracotta warriors which were excavated in Xian in China, the other two, a general and an officer stand guard over the Secret Garden.

A high granite wall at the back of the long west facing border offers protection to tender and unusual plants including *Solanum jasminoides* 'Album', *Azara dentata, Carpenteria californica, Cassia corymbosa, Acca sellowiana* which has fleshy red and white edible petals with long crimson stamens, *Stauntonia hexaphylla* which also produces edible purple tinged fruits after a warm dry summer, and *Dregea sinensis* with deliciously scented white flowers.

Through an opening in the long wall is the tennis court edged with crab apples and the vegetable garden. Mostly grown from seed, crops produce an abundant supply for the household including lettuce, Jerusalem artichokes, rhubarb, blackberries and wineberries. For picking, *Alstroemeria* 'Princess' hybrids provide long lasting cut flowers.

Borders generally are fluid in their design and planted with trees and shrubs, many originating from China including *Acer davidii, Itea ilicifolia, Neillia thibetica* and *Osmanthus delavayi*. Particularly fond of buddlejas, both for their fragrance and for the multitude of butterflies that they attract, Lady Brownlow's collection includes some of the

more unusual forms, *Buddleja lindleyana, B. fallowiana* var. *'Alba', B. davidii* 'Black Knight' and *B. crispa* whose velvety stems and leaves are coated in white felt. Other beds are filled with sun-loving and aromatic plants such as *Phlomis italica, Parahebe perfoliata, Caryopteris* x *clandonensis* 'Heavenly Blue', rosemary and sage.

Throughout, there is evidence of the subtle artistry in which Lady Brownlow has affectionately arranged and grouped plants in her remarkable garden.

A DRAMATIC HEADLAND

Situated on a rocky promontory surrounded by the Atlantic sea is a unique garden whose boundaries are the high water mark. There are no lawns (except for one tiny patch) instead the sea creates a magnificent vista engulfing the whole site and offering breathtaking views.

Until the original house was built in 1924 all that could be seen on the headland were the Napoleonic defences built around 1810 using excavated granite from a quarry which now forms part of the Wild Garden. These included the double open fort, granite arsenal (which is now a cottage) crenellated wall and the guard house on top of the hill. The concrete bunkers (one of which has been converted into a garden shed) and the roof over the fort were built by the Germans during the Occupation when they commandeered the property.

facing page: *The brilliantly exploding colour of magenta and pink ice-plants (that is so surprising to find in nature) contrasts with the mellow tones of the granite and the bright azure blue of the sea.*

Robin and Pam Forbes, bought the house in 1988 completely rebuilding it and extending a terrace out over the sea. About 1,000 tons of rock and shale were removed, and extensive restoration work was necessary to the walls and terraces around the garden.

There is an all pervading sense of the power of the sea; the sounds, smells and changing colours from deep slate grey to bright azure – heaven from early summer to late autumn, but in the winter, the merciless salt-laden winds can be very bleak,

howling through the garden, violent gusts burning all but the toughest foliage. In front of the house tree purslane, *Atriplex halimus,* gives shelter together with a tall bay, that is growing up from a crevice just above sea level. An oddity at first sight are the stocks which self-sow each year on the rocks below and in late winter *Narcissus* 'Paper White' give a brave display spilling over the banks down to the sea. Nearby are the rubble remains of what may have been a goat house.

Along the main path plants struggle to survive in the shallow sandy soil. A narrow border is planted with windbreak shrubs including *Elaeagnus ebbingei,* escallonia and the strawberry tree, *Arbutus unedo*. Surprisingly, several 'American Pillar' roses flower profusely despite the conditions.

The Southern tip of the headland bears the full brunt of the elements and holm oaks are tortured and twisted by the continual onslaught of the wind, although the juvenile foliage conceals the contorted branches and coarse leathery leaves of previous years growth. The hurricane of 1987 and further storms in 1991 brought down many of the large

Monterey pines, *Pinus radiata,* exposing the garden even more. It took weeks to clear the damage, as restricted access made it impossible to use machinery, but now natural regeneration is occurring and seedlings emerge only a few centimetres away from young trees. The owners are particularly keen to conserve the natural vegetation and throughout the garden wild flowers are allowed to self-sow at will. There are over 140 grasses and wild flowers recorded including Sheep's-bit, Great Quaking grass, Portland spurge, sea radish and a small-flowered evening primrose.

Overlooking the horseshoe-shaped bay below, the robust hottentot-fig rampages over the cliff face but within the garden control is essential as this triffid like invader can quickly smother and kill other vegetation. On a sunny day its bright yellow flowers

facing page left: *Wild flowers are allowed to self-sow at will and help to conserve the natural vegetation and compatible wildlife.*

facing page top right: *Wild flowers mingle on the cliff face overlooking the horseshoe-shaped bay below and green lizards scuttle out from their hiding places to bask on the rocks.*

facing page bottom right: *On a sunny day, dazzled by the wonderful view, you forget just how powerful and aggressive the salt-laden winds can be.*

look dramatic against the magenta and pink ice-plants *(Lampranthus* and *Mesembryanthemum)* providing a vivid splash of colour. Seagulls peck at the shoots and remove bits as nesting material as green lizards scuttle out from their hiding places to bask on the rocks. After flowering all succulents are dead-headed with shears leaving just a few to self-sow.

Through a decorative wrought iron gate and enclosed by a granite wall and tough, drought resistant planting, the Sheltered Garden is distinctly different. The colours and textures are subtle and muted; furry greys, olive green, sage, and soft mauves woven together in a tapestry effect. With its own microclimate the temperature can

above: *The Sheltered Garden has its own microclimate and many of the plants that flourish here have Mediterranean origins. A purple berberis and New Zealand cabbage palm,* Cordyline australis, *are dominant features amongst the many rock roses, brooms and aromatic herbs.*

soar to 140 degrees Fahrenheit in the shade and many of the plants that flourish here have Mediterranean origins, such as the tree mallows, *Lavatera olbia* and *Phlomis fruticosa* which flower freely throughout the summer. Aromatic herbs, rock roses and brooms jostle happily together often growing in the same planting pocket and *Lavandula stoechas,* which disappeared from the higher banks, now colonise cracks between the granite crazy paving. Other plants that revel in the sun-baked conditions include the South African Cape marigold, *Dimorphotheca* and *Callistemon citrinus* 'Splendens' from Australia with dense cylindrical bottlebrush spikes of red flowers.

In late summer the terrace overlooking the Sheltered Garden becomes too intense with the heat that radiates off the sun drenched granite but early in the year it is wonderful and has even been used for lunch in December. The cliff behind gives wind protection and on a sunny winter's day this terrace can be completely sheltered in total contrast to the other side of the garden.

The brick built pergola and terrace date from the early 1920's and it is a continual struggle to find adaptable climbers that can cope with the wind once they have reached the top. Rambling roses such as 'Paul's Himalayan Musk' and 'Rambling Rector' do well, but the solanums are cut back by the elements each winter although the blue form, *Solanum crispum* 'Glasnevin' appears to be the toughest.

There are many bunkers throughout the garden and concealing them has become quite an art; some are camouflaged with Virginia creeper, others have been cleverly disguised by adding soil to the roof and softened with cascading plants.

Stepping out from one of these dark enclosures, sunlight filtering through large *Cupressus macrocarpa* emphasises the dramatic tiered carpet of ice-plants that flow lava-like down the rock face, giving the impression of a luxuriant lawn without the need for mowing and when the flowers expand in sunshine the massed effect becomes all the more spectacular. A garden is never static and although frosts are rare, a severe winter could bring devastation to all the succulents.

Narrow paths perilously mount the almost vertical rock face to the guard house; the scream of gulls and the sound of the

above: *Narrow paths mount the rock face through the dramatic tiered carpet of ice-plants that flow like lava, giving the impression of a luxuriant lawn.*

waves can be heard crashing onto the rocks far below. These higher reaches were denuded of vegetation until little snippets were introduced into rock crevices which have spread rapidly to form broad bands of interest. The trailing snapdragon, *Asarina procumbens* with pale creamy flowers was discovered tucked under a bush and is now self-sowing happily, and the unusual and somewhat treacherous *Fascicularia pitcairniifolia* has secured several positions along the path; particularly striking at the end of the summer when the ninety centimetre long narrow spiny leaves form a rosette from which develop red bracts around a central cluster of blue flowers.

From the guard house a path leads through a small wooded area and meanders down behind the house into the Wild Garden where, protected from the salt winds a solitary camellia, evergreen azaleas and hydrangeas mingle with ferns, foxgloves and primroses, providing a cool retreat on a hot summer's day.

This remarkable creation has evolved through experimentation, determination and the perseverance of two gardeners who rise to a challenge and enjoy everyday eye contact with the landscape that they love.

This property has now changed hands.

41

AFTER THE GREAT STORM

Set against a rugged cliff face lit by wild gorse is 'Westward'. Built in 1928, it has spectacular
views across to the parish church, rectory and the generous sweep of
St Brelade's Bay.

Mayda and the late Major Jacque Reynolds bought the house in 1970 inheriting with it, a
labour intensive garden of terraces and gravel paths. The Great Storm of 1987 (to which
there is now a memorial gate) brought with it almost total devastation forcing a complete
re-think about both its design and maintenance. A shelterbelt of giant *Cupressus macrocarpa*
were totally uprooted as was the blue cedar that dominated the front façade.

A staunch survivor of the lower garden is a black walnut, *Juglans nigra,* withstanding the
force of the gale, its roots firmly anchored in the stream that flows through the garden
and out to sea.

It took six months of intensive labour to clear the debris and to bring in mammoth quantities of topsoil to fill the large craters, the result of one night of destruction. Now, forty eight imposing lime trees, *Tilia* x *euchlora,* border the south and west boundaries.

facing page: *A camellia and flamboyant azalea make a colourful foil to a stone lantern.*

above: *Moisture-loving perennials are planted in impressive blocks drawing the eye to the pond.*

left, bottom left & bottom right*: Mayda Reynolds is passionate about camellias. These form some of the large collection.*

Past president of the International Camellia Society, Mayda Reynolds has a lavish collection of over one hundred and forty five camellias in her four acre garden. Together with Manuel who has helped tirelessly for over two decades, rhododendrons, azaleas, camellias and hydrangeas are tucked into every available corner particularly along the entrance drive where they thrive in the acid conditions and amongst the woodland behind the house, where narrow paths allow access to the steep terraces.

The time to appreciate the collection in all its infinite variety is between early and late spring when the display is at its peak although the season extends from as early as October. Blooms range from the small single flowers of *C.* 'Cornish Snow' to the dinner-plate sized flowers of *C.* 'Lasca Beauty' (Mayda's favourite) and *C. reticulata* 'Captain Rawes' and from the fragrant *C. sasanqua* 'Narumi-gata' to the exquisitely formed miniature flowers of *C.* 'Spring Festival'. Mayda's interest in camellias has taken her to many places, including Japan, Australia, New Zealand and the United States and a visit to China provided some rare seedlings which are being nurtured including *Camellia lapidea, C. nitidissimma,* and *C. villosa.*

To the east side of the house procumbent roses bloom with spectacular freedom including the 'The Fairy' roses with dense clusters of delicate pink flowers and in summer the south facing Mediterranean borders come into their own. These large sloping borders immediately infront of the house are planted with sun-lovers, mainly grey foliage plants and spiky exotics that revel in the dry acid sand. *Eucalyptus johnstonii, E. nicholii* and cordylines rise above hummocks of artemisias, cistus such as *C. lusitanicus, C. ladanifer* and *C.* x *aguilari* 'Maculatus', hebes, *Lavandula stoechas* and osteospermums.

Sweeping lawns follow the natural contours down to the lower garden. Here, perennials swell the borders surrounding the pond and stream. Planted in large blocks to give impact from a distance, bold clumps of bamboo, globe thistles, *Echinops ritro* and arum lilies rival great drifts of mahogany leaved, *Ligularia dentata* 'Desdemona', *Eupatorium purpureum* and *E. rugosum, Iris sibirica* 'Perry's Blue', astilbe and tricyrtis. Geraniums in variety form thick carpets at ground level including *G. ibericum,*

facing page: *A constant reminder of 'The Great Storm' this gate comes to life in late summer when a passion flower,* Passiflora caerulea *and a cup-and-saucer vine,* Cobaea scandens *are at their best.*

below: *White tobacco plants,* Nicotiana sylvestris *are a delight when they come into flower. Here they appear illuminated in the slanting sun rays.*

G. macrorrhizum 'Ingwersen's Variety', *G.* x *cantabrigiense* and *G.* x *oxonianum* 'Claridge Druce'. The oak-leaved hydrangea, *Hydrangea quercifolia* and the eye catching stems of the dogwoods, *Cornus alba* 'Sibirica' and *C. stolonifera* 'Flaviramea' extend the display through the autumn and into the winter and offer cover for the numerous permanent and visiting wildfowl which add a constant flurry of activity.

The Great Storm caused much destruction but out of it Mayda has developed a beautiful garden that is a joy for all to see.

There are several ways to arrive at the manor grounds but the most impressive is through the elaborate black and gold gates that were forged in Italy. Straight ahead is the new Main Drive. Future generations will be able to benefit from the planted avenue that will mature into a magnificent lime drive in a style befitting the grandeur and tradition of the estate. John Dick acquired 'St John's Manor' twenty years ago and has masterminded much of the restoration of the grounds including the main lawn and lake in front of the house and the Japanese Garden.

WATER AND STATUARY

facing page: *Beneath the tall canopy of a stand of sycamores, small deer accentuate the contrast in scale.*

The garden is made up of a number of different complementary spaces. Beyond the swimming pool and tennis court is a dark shady grove of rhododendrons and laurel. The lack of light creates an environment that precludes the use of any underplanting but a hammock is suspended between two trees providing a cool retreat on a hot summer's day.

Skirting the drive, just before the chapel and on the opposite side, is a stand of tall sycamores whose crowns have been lifted creating a surreal picture. Their trunks rise up to the sky, small deer emphasise the contrast in scale and shafts of sunlight create a theatrical atmosphere.

The chapel, on the left of the Main Drive, was built by May Raworth in memory of her late husband, Alexander Spreckley Raworth, Seigneur of Saint Jean who died in 1950. Inside, can be seen an unusual carving of St John the Baptist, created from a single tree trunk. From a stone bench backed by a semi-circular yew hedge, you can absorb the grand scale of the parkland, the physical presence of the manor house, an imposing purple beech and the graceful shadows cast over the lake.

far left: *The woven bamboo fence around the Japanese Garden creates a feeling of security, rocks give a sense of stability and the sound of water dripping from the bamboo pipe helps to restore the inner calm and peace of mind.*

middle left: *An imposing Buddha oversees the tranquillity of the scene.*

below: *Through stillness and reflection, the expanse of water unites the garden with the sky.*

Opposite the boathouse and the main lake is the Japanese Garden. With strong visual appeal even in the winter through the use of water, boulders and evergreens, it is an oasis for meditation and contemplation. As you enter through the gateway note the perfectly raked gravel set with *Echeveria elegans*. Here there is a desire for peace and serenity, for a quiet place of at least transient solitude and solace.

As in nature, there is a balance of unity and asymmetry in the use of water, rocks and plants. Elements are opposing and yet harmonious; space and form, coarse and fine textures, light and dark, vertical and horizontal. There is a sense of security and enclosure created by a woven bamboo fence and yet the canopy of surrounding trees creates a feeling of depth and distance. Through reflection, the water unites the garden with the sky and stepping stones taking you on a visual as well as a physical journey. The bridge, set to be viewed on the diagonal creates a sense of enlarged space and then there is the sound of

top right:
Classical statues are used as focal points amongst dark evergreens or to draw the eye to the end of a vista.

bottom right:
Almost hidden, in a shady corner is the Hougue. A narrow winding path entices the visitor to the top.

far right:
Viewed across the lake, the manor house glows in the afternoon twilight of a winter's day.

water dripping from a bamboo pipe. Choice of plants is restricted, many are clipped to shape including conifers, camellias and bamboos. Maples and a weeping cherry contrast with the clouds of Kurume azaleas which are massed around the water's edge and surrounding banks and a wisteria scrambles up to the top of an old tree.

Leaving the Japanese Garden, you will enjoy a successive series of views across the main lake and its spraying fountain. Chusan palms, *Trachycarpus fortunei*, (many over seventy years old) form an avenue and impressive statues are set against dark yew and holly providing a certain rhythm.

Across the broad expanse of lawn is a gazebo and almost hidden in the shrubbery beyond is the Hougue, an extraordinary moss covered mound which tempts both adults and children alike to reach the top. Again, you are aware of the play of light and shade as you emerge to see the house bathed in full sun. At the back of the manor is the walled kitchen garden and a duck pond, much less formal and always a scene of activity and excitement.

As time passes it will be the grandeur, water and classical statuary of St John's Manor that will linger in your memory.

A PAINTER'S PALETTE

Ariel and Richard Whatmore live in an ancient granite house hidden deep in the countryside and approached by a long tree-lined avenue.

On arrival you will see a small gravel courtyard where walls are colonised by self-sowing daisies, *Erigeron karvinskianus* and white doves emerge from the rafters of an open barn. A north facing corner is filled with young camellias including *C.* 'Cornish Snow', *C.* 'Hugh Evans' and the unusual *Camellia campsii*. In summer, pots overflow with pink geraniums some of which remain outside all year and have formed huge architectural mounds. Immediately you are aware of a comforting sense of intimacy and peaceful seclusion.

The enchanting views from 'Les Aix', part of which dates back to 1432, liberate the spirit. Divided by only a ha-ha, the strong central axis from the front door visually extends beyond a row of pleached limes and a charming sculpture to the open meadowland beyond. As an artist specialising in the painting of gardens, it is fitting that Ariel has combined formal design elements using perfectly clipped box and topiary with an expressive blending of character, shape and texture. Washes of colour progress through from predominantly white to the sunny yellows of pineapple broom, *Cytisus battandieri* and hummocks of silver santolina and on to the muted pinks and misty mauves of *Lavatera bicolor*, buddlejas and catmint. A great swag of the vibrant rose 'Dorothy Perkins' frames the front door and fills the house with its sweet perfume. On the far side of the garden, alternate plain and variegated ivies dress the trunks of a row of pleached limes and contrast with a fine weeping elm and the sentinel yews.

Underplanted with a tapestry of white valerian and poppies, a sundial, a recent acquisition, is embraced with cuttings of yew, which in time will be cut into a crenellated hedge.

above: *A charming sculpture is used as a focal point to draw the eye along a box-edged path.*

facing page: *Clipped yew and box give symmetry to the front entrance.*

Leading up to the Nut Walk is a spring border. A delight early in the year when hundreds of snowdrops and crocus bravely poke through the frozen ground, joined by aconites which do not favour the acid conditions of Jersey soil. "We feed them lime like crazy" says Ariel. These are followed by *Anemone blanda* and epimediums and then later by foxgloves and osteospermums creating a border of wild abandonment.

An opening in the wall highlighted by a discerning arch of Portugal laurel, reveals a secret retreat known as the Cottage Garden. In winter, structure is provided by clipped hebes and *Daphne odora* 'Aureomarginata' that grow profusely, planted in granite troughs. In summer, orange, red and yellow flowers explode to give a fiery display.

At the back of the house raised borders are designed to give foliage interest throughout the year with two large weeping pears, *Pyrus salicifolia* 'Pendula' guarding the central steps. A purple smoke tree and B*erberis thunbergii* 'Rose Glow', complement catmint, senecio and phlomis and are seasoned with splashes of acid *Euphorbia cyparissias* and the lime flowers of lady's mantle. *Convolvulus cneorum* spills over the wall and *Erigeron karvinskianus* seeds into every crack. Below in the fine gravel, *Helleborus lividus corsicus*, wallflowers and valerian are allowed to self-sow at will whilst pots of bay and Christmas box, *Sarcococca confusa,* give solidity and structure.

The Nut Walk on the other hand is underplanted with shade-loving hostas and hellebores, *Helleborus orientalis* which flower in a range of luscious shades from pink to velvety plum and deep dusky purple. Primroses and polyanthus adore the conditions and form a thick blanket. You are drawn along beneath the catkin-laden hazels enticed by an unusual seat made by Andrew Garten which is backed by a yew hedge topped with a topiarised pheasant. Emergence from shade into bright light heightens the contrast.

Skirting a group of trees in grass, including a strawberry tree and winter flowering cherry, you will encounter the swimming pool and tennis court. Beds are filled with old roses with such romantic names as 'Boule de Neige', 'Fantin Latour', 'Desprez à Fleurs Jaunes' and 'Blush Noisette' and are underplanted with penstemons and feverfew, providing a glorious show all summer long.

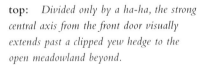

top: *Divided only by a ha-ha, the strong central axis from the front door visually extends past a clipped yew hedge to the open meadowland beyond.*

middle left: *The Cottage Garden seen through an ancient arch looks serene in winter but in summer explodes in a riot of bright colours.*

middle right: *Inside the Cottage Garden, bright yellow* Euryops pectinatus *add a touch of sunshine on a December day.*

bottom right: Iris unguicularis *adds a splash of colour at the base of a high granite wall.*

All gardens should have an element of surprise and this one is no exception. Totally unexpected and hidden behind a yew hedge is a maze designed by Randoll Coate. Planted in the shape of an artist's palette, box hedging (all grown from cuttings) defines the grain whilst flowers become symbolic pools of colour; purple, pink, yellow, green and blue. Intimate and completely personal, the letters in Ariel's name are also represented; alliums, roses, iris, euphorbia, and lobelia. Each flower bed is punctuated by a simple but solid clipped standard bay. The centre is a circle of water reflecting the house name 'Les Aix' or 'The Waters'.

The Kitchen Garden provides vegetables for the table; artichokes, sweetcorn and beans together with a bountiful supply of fruit; raspberries, blackcurrants and

gooseberries. Next to it is a peaceful triangular corner enclosed by a beech hedge and planted with a sprinkling of trees. A recent project is the planting of an orchard of cider apple cultivars.

Heading back to the courtyard through a tiny seating area where a central pot and cordyline add a tropical touch, you will pass a long herbaceous border loosely planted under the influence of Jekyll's colour theory; starting with cool tones rising to hotter yellows and reds in the middle and then fading to soft mauves and purples.

In this garden there is an atmosphere of peace and harmony created by an artist's vision.

At 'Le Clos du Chemin' half hardy exotics flourish, cushioned by the warmth of the house walls. A magnificent *Brugmansia sanguinea*, three metres tall, spans the same width, whilst nearby is a lush tangle of *Clematis armandii* and tucked into a sheltered corner is a pale blue plumbago. Pots of scented plants crowd the open porch in front of the house including the wonderfully fragrant *Rhododendron* 'Fragrantissimum'.

Inheriting the house and garden about twelve years ago, Sue Lea is a plantswoman who enjoys seeking out the unusual and who manages to recreate just the right microclimate necessary. Some of these plants can be found near the loggia. Here the air is filled with honey-scented *Euphorbia mellifera* and Mediterranean plants such as *Olearia phlogopappa*, shrubby rock roses, *Hebe hulkeana* and *Correa lawrenceana* with felted leaves and seductive nodding blooms in soft greenish-cream often flowering all through the winter. A broom, *Cytisus proliferus* flowers early, grown from seed brought back from La Gomera in the Canary Islands.

Silver borders edge the terrace, filled with lavender, sage, blue rue, *Ballota pseudodictamnus* and *Artemisia arborescens* 'Faith Raven' and gold and silver plants continue the theme along a path that runs the length of the garden including *Euonymus fortunei* 'Emerald 'n' Gold', yellow and white potentillas and *Spiraea japonica* 'Goldflame'.

UNSUSPECTED TREASURES

Screening shrubs offer privacy from a neighbouring property and a background to the purple, gold and grey plantings on The Long Border. Here flower *Magnolia* 'Vulcan', the darkest of reds and *M.* 'Apollo' with rosy red flowers shading to purple. An accidental pairing of gold helichrysum and ceanothus creates a woven tapestry and a log store is cleverly hidden behind a hedge of purple beech underplanted with clumps of *Houttuynia cordata* 'Chameleon'.

Quite different in character, the lower garden is planted with shade-loving camellias and rhododendrons including *R.* 'Loderi King George', the fragrant *R. diaprepes* and the very beautiful *R.* 'Fabia' with funnel-shaped scarlet and apricot flowers shaded with brown speckles. Other shrubs include *Stuartia pseudocamellia* var. *koreana*, *Hoheria angustifolia* and *Vestia foetida* which bears an abundance of pale yellow tubular flowers from mid-spring to mid-summer. Maples including *Acer palmatum* 'Osakazuki' and *A. p.* 'Senkaki'

enjoy the cool canopy provided by *Aesculus indica* 'Sydney Pearce' and hellebores, hosta, and *Tellima grandiflora* are pierced in spring by clumps of daffodils. Another wonderful combination are the *Paulownia tomentosa* and *Koelreuteria paniculata* that rise above sheets of bluebells.

The late Robert Lea had a passion for magnolias and there are now numerous varieties to be found in the garden, some having magnificent large flowers in tones of purple to pink, others with tiny ones such as the unusual *M. stellata* 'Chrysanthemiflora'. The popular *M. liliiflora* 'Nigra' is one which Sue values for its long flowering period. There are also several yellow flowered forms including *M.* 'Yellow Bird' with greenish-yellow blooms and *M. denudata* 'Elizabeth'.

An arbour constructed as a millennium project is host to a Japanese honeysuckle, a tender *Araujia sericifera*, *Clematis forsteri* and *Pandorea pandorana* and gaps from honey fungus casualties are quickly replanted with aspiring newcomers.

facing page: *Luxuriant growth around a classical column.*

top: *A sensational wisteria is pruned regularly to maintain its shape.*

middle left: *A delicious mix of lily of the valley and white polyanthus.*

middle right: *Self sown* Geranium maderense, *with a mat of houseleeks.*

bottom: *Music in the air amid strongly aromatic rosemary.*

The hidden Italianate Garden is planted in silver and white, accessible only through a wisteria-clad archway flanked by huge hummocks of cistus. Planting is kept to a minimum around the simple geometric lines. A rectangular water lily pond edged with gravel, encompasses the centre stage terminating at one end in a trompe-l'oeil, mirrored to reflect the symmetry. At the opposite end is a segmented semi-circle of box filled with aromatic foliage, punctuated in spring by *Tulipa* 'Spring Green'. Glaucous eucalyptus grown from seed contrast with *Acacia rhetinodes* and *A. baileyana* 'Purpurea', variegated box grown from cuttings are clipped into shape and the green columns of *Cupressus sempervirens* add a distinct presence.

Throughout the year the Italianate Garden plays on your emotions but remains a place of calm, whilst borders bulge

facing page: *Reflection in the Italianate Garden.*

left: Helleborus lividus corsicus *sparkles in the winter sunshine.*

right: *Hidden behind a decorative gate is the Italianate Garden.*

with mixed plantings and hidden delights that, in spring, burst into life when every day brings forth a new surprise or unsuspected treasure.

A ROMANTIC

HIDEAWAY

Hidden behind a large granite archway is a secret garden, a sanctuary in which to dream away the hours, a refuge in which to revitalise one's soul. 'Mont Pellier' is a charming granite house, dating from 1640, set in a picturesque valley and once the home of the Pellier family. When Barbara and the late Roy Overland acquired the house in 1985 they were fortunate to also inherit a wonderful garden that had been laid out over thirty years by the previous owners, John and the late Mary Best.

Quintessentially a romantic country garden echoing all that is enchanting and magical but with the addition of inspired touches made by the Overlands, reminiscent of the warm scents and colours of Provence. With their own individual style, they have introduced delightful decorative elements - large pots, brought back from Provence in warm earthy tones that now overflow with *Melianthus major* and bronze sculptures, that are cleverly sited in shady corners.

Groves of trees and shrubs were planted to give a woodland effect and now provide a magnificent green backdrop of birch, oak,

left: *An idyllic corner,* Libertia formosa *and* Meconopsis cambrica *surrounding a warm terracotta pot overflowing with* Melianthus major.

right: *The covering of snow gives luminosity to this tranquil setting, making an almost monochome picture.*

cherries, maples, *Cercidiphyllum japonicum, Fagus* var. *heterophylla* 'Aspleniifolia', the graceful cut-leaf beech which is so rarely planted in gardens and the pink flowered horse chestnut, *Aesculus* x *carnea* 'Briottii'. Perimeter borders were planted thickly using gently curving outlines and massed with rhododendrons, camellias, pieris and *Enkianthus campanulatus.* Wide grass walkways, now mossy under the heavy tree canopy, bestow a romantic atmosphere and are carpeted with naturalised bulbs; daffodils, bluebells and *Leucojum aestivum.* In spring, leafy glades are illuminated with the miniature *Narcissus cyclamineus* 'Tête-à-Tête' creating enormous pools of pure gold.

At the entrance, evergreen azaleas are restrained by a low box hedge and together with *Anemone nemorosa* 'Robinsoniana' provide a spectacular display under the protective canopy of acers and magnolias. An old apple crusher, originally used for pressing cider apples, is bedded out twice yearly with colourful displays of annuals and spring bulbs. Just visible, a brick-edged gravel path disappears beyond a dense planting of lacecap hydrangeas underplanted with lamium and bluebells through a wooden gate to the beehives beyond from which excellent honey is produced.

top: *Towards the end of autumn, the whole garden glows in orange, scarlet and gold. Collecting the fallen leaves is a major task.*

bottom: *Autumn is distinguished by myriad coloured leaves as they fall and settle on the apple crusher at the entrance.*

The garden comes alive early in the year when the dainty species *Narcissus cyclamineus* pierce the mossy carpet under the bole of a huge London plane producing an alluring tapestry with blue *Anemone blanda* – a heart warming picture on chilly days. By the end of May the garden is alight with flame coloured azaleas. Along the drive they produce a glowing array of sunset colours, crimson, scarlet, tangerine and apricot yellow including the Knaphill hybrids, 'Lady Rosebery', 'Rumba' and 'Wryneck' and Ghent hybrids 'Nancy Waterer' and 'William III'.

A route has to be carefully chosen up the grass slope to the Camellia Walk so as not to disturb the profusion of sparkling blue *Chionodoxa luciliae*. Flourishing in the acid soil conditions and filtered sunlight, *Camellia* x *williamsii* hybrids join with *Camellia japonica* to give a lengthy flowering period from early November until the end of May. Colours range from the blush

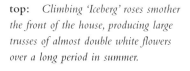

top: *Climbing 'Iceberg' roses smother the front of the house, producing large trusses of almost double white flowers over a long period in summer.*

middle: *A vivid scarlet azalea entices the visitor to explore further into the garden.*

bottom: *There is an understated charm and incomparable seasonal beauty of Rhododendron luteum reflected in the still water of the pond infront of the house.*

pink of 'Elizabeth de Rothschild' and 'Charles Michael' through to the clear pink of 'Berenice Boddy' and the bright red of 'Adolphe Audusson'. In April, magnolias lighten the scene with their attractive spreading habit and white ribbony flowers.

Near the lake (which is home to tufted ducks, winter visitors who return each year) is a wonderful specimen cherry, its branches weighing heavily with blossom in May when it spreads its canopy over bold swathes of bluebells. Close by a billowing white *Clematis montana* reaches high into the branches of a fine blue cedar, *Cedrus atlantica* Glauca Form.

In summer climbing 'Iceberg' roses smother the front of the house with the slow growing *Rhaphiolepsis* x *delacourii* and *Carpenteria californica* camouflaging their feet and a flamboyant pink rose with exceptionally large blousy flowers making a vivid centre piece clambering over the wellhead.

In front of the terrace low box hedging punctuated by bold box spheres and cones gives a sturdy framework to the hazy profusion and lax abandonment of summery white flowers such as *Penstemon* 'Snow Storm', *Viola cornuta* 'Alba', *Phlox subulata* 'White Delight', *Scabiosa caucasica* 'Miss. Willmott', delphiniums and dwarf agapanthus.

The lawn slopes gently down to a pond which is richly planted with flowering shrubs and moisture-loving perennials that are mirrored in the still water. Ferns thrive in the dappled shade of the surrounding banks and a creeper-clad pergola has become home to unusual shade-loving treasures including *Smilacina stellata*, *Hacquetia epipactis*, *Actaea pachypoda*, *Fritillaria affinis*, *Trillium luteum* and *Erythronium revolutum* 'White Beauty'.

Two bronze deer draw the eye to a group of azaleas and August flowering hibiscus just beyond a stunning specimen *Cornus controversa* 'Variegata'.

A small courtyard linked to the breakfast room, has been designed to give interest all year, with an intricate pattern of Italian marble cobbles, French granite setts and yorkstone. In summer it becomes an outdoor room for entertaining and

above: *A cherry tree makes a glorious sight in May.*

right: *Bronze deer look serene resting under the canopy of tall hornbeams.*

facing page: *Under the arching branches of a beautiful weeping willow, colourful azaleas soften the pond edge.*

relaxing. The beds overflow with flowers the colour of sunshine including the rich yellow rose 'Graham Thomas', one of David Austin's wonderful English roses, and golden dwarf daylilies, *Hemerocallis* 'Eenie Weenie', lemon *Anthemis* 'E.C. Buxton' and *Coreopsis* 'Zagreb', all highlighted with touches of white from delphiniums, agapanthus and Japanese anemones. Yellow flowered *Cassia corymbosa* enjoy the protection of the

warm granite walls and the sweet jasmine-like fragrance of *Trachelospermum asiaticum* fills the air with scent throughout the summer.

Mont Pellier is a garden that arouses all of one's senses; appealing to one's emotions, mixing elements of surprise with a carefree informality in the true romantic tradition.

Le Coin, the home of Brenda, Lady Cook, has a colourful history. Originally a farm with outbuildings, dating in part back to the early 17th century. The main house was built in 1760 with subsequent additions and modifications added over the years.

When Sir Francis and Lady Cook arrived in Jersey in the early 1950's, the forecourt with the fountain was a farmyard and the lower garden, surrounded by high retaining walls, was wild with just a few fruit trees and a stream. But the late Sir Francis

IN THE MANNER OF MONSERRATE

could see a resemblance to Monserrate in Sintra, Portugal, which was once part of the family estate, where he must have had many happy memories of childhood journeys to its magnificent gardens which were substantially developed by his ancestors.

At Monserrate, the house is set in vast acres built at the top of a steep spur with panoramic views and lawns that run down to a lake. Le Coin is a fraction of the size but Sir Francis had the idea of copying it a little, capturing the ambiance of the place, albeit on a miniature scale. At Le Coin there are two full-time gardeners, at Monserrate, in its hey day, there were seventy two!

right: *View from the Long Walk back towards the house. Stately pampas grass,* Cortaderia selloana *punctuate the end of this part of the walk. In late summer, erect plume-like silvery panicles are produced and last well into the winter.*

left: *Red hollyhocks, an old-fashioned and much loved perennial make a bright composition in front of a hardy fuschia,* Fuschia magellanica *'Riccartonii'*

Since 1956 the late Sir Francis and Lady Cook have made many alterations both to the house and the garden, creating a small park with a magnolia plantation, a kitchen garden, the 'Becquet' on the opposite side of the road, a new entrance drive and borders structured on different levels.

A magnificent purple beech overhangs the entrance and in its season the magnolia plantation reliably rewards with a spectacular display. *Magnolia grandiflora* 'Goliath' line the drive and provide a dark glossy backcloth against which deciduous varieties sparkle including *M. wilsonii* with pendulous, saucer-shaped, fragrant white flowers, *M.* x *thompsoniana* with huge fragrant flowers the colour of parchment, *M.* 'Heaven Scent' and the aristocratic *M.* x *soulangeana* 'Brozzonii', one of the largest-flowered and the latest of the group to bloom.

Tucked away, is the swimming pool. Colourful in summer when procumbent roses afford a flamboyant show of reds, pinks and whites. Many belong to the wonderful County series such as *Rosa* 'Wiltshire', *R.* 'Northamptonshire' and *R.* 'Surrey'.

The herbaceous border produces a tapestry of harmonious colours, shapes and textures. A few shrubs through the middle, give height and winter interest but it is in the summer that this long sumptuous border peaks in tones of peachy pink, blue and white. Diascias, rock roses and pinks are offset by campanulas, delphiniums and scabious, sharpened here and there by patches of deep crimson and coral penstemons and spiked by the tall plumes of *Stipa gigantea* strategically positioned along its length. Narrow steps descend to parallel borders where large clumps of sturdy agapanthus contrast with hazy catmint.

The Long Walk skilfully combines gold and silver foliage and grasses; feathery *Artemisia* 'Powys Castle' with the gold grass-like *Acorus gramineus* 'Ogon'; *Physocarpus opulifolius* 'Dart's Gold' with *Lavandula stoechas; Convolvulus cneorum* with the whipcord *Hebe armstrongii* and as architectural statements are a pair of *Cordyline* 'Torbay Dazzler'. Two large pampas grasses mark the end of this walk but a statue beckons beyond. New Zealand flax, *Phormium tenax* 'Purpureum' positioned intermittently along a narrow border create an exciting visual effect interplanted with textural foliage including *Pulmonaria saccharata* Argentea Group, *Taxus baccata* 'Fastigiata', *Prunus laurocerasus* 'Otto Luyken' and *Hebe rakaiensis.*

From the house, which is draped in climbers and creepers, is a birds-eye view over the valley. A decorative wrought iron gate swings open revealing a steep flight of steps that descend to the lily pond. The balustrade is smothered by honeysuckle that pervades the evening air as it scrambles over the stone. An ageing fig fans out against a high retaining wall, monopolising all the available space, its trunk gnarled and twisted, masked in summer by a subtropical-looking *Melianthus major.* Angel's trumpets, *Brugmansia sanguinea* enjoy a sheltered corner and have reached huge proportions remaining in the open ground all year, protected by surrounding shrubs.

A magnolia and camellia border extends the whole length of the roadside wall and is underplanted with colourful grasses and architectural plants. Opposite, two fastigiate yew stand sentinel either side of steep steps, a short-cut to the Long Walk.

Spring water gently flows into a series of tiered pools culminating in a lily pond. Frogs are camouflaged, spiky tufts

of *Iris sibirica* and small leaf hostas break the edge and magnificent clumps of *Zantedeschia aethiopica* display their waxy white spathes for several months in early summer. A seat, a refuge from the outside world, is carefully positioned; the perfect spot to inspect the minutia of the pond and to admire the view back up to the house.

Trees and shrubs form the backbone and extend the visual impact through to the winter including *Crinodendron hookerianum* stunning in flower with its pendulous coral lanterns, *Fatsia japonica,* the coral bark maple, *Acer palmatum* 'Senkaki', and *Robinia pseudoacacia* 'Frisia' backlit by the evening sun. There is a gentle transition from the formal garden to the naturalised planting giving an illusion of infinity.

Leaving behind the wilder areas of the valley garden a narrow path ascends under the shady woodland canopy opening out into the sunlit expanse of the Kitchen Garden. Until recently, this south facing *côtil* provided the household with early crops of Jersey Royal potatoes together with globe artichokes, asparagus, sweetcorn and spinach. Cut flowers for the house are still grown in rows including *Alstroemeria* hybrids, sweet williams, Jersey lilies, *Amaryllis belladonna,* peonies, gladioli, lilies and sweetpeas. Lily of the valley romps around the entrance to one of the glasshouses which are used to over winter half hardy shrubs and houseplants including a wonderful collection of orchids.

This is a garden that is a poignant echo of an idealised past and one might like to think captures some of the spirit of Monserrate and the vision and memories of past travels.

top left: *A synthesis of colour - blue agapanthus and yellow lilies.*

top right: *A cup-and-saucer vine,* Cobaea scandens *produces masses of flowers that open yellow-green and age to purple.*

bottom left: *A decorative wrought iron gate swings open revealing a steep flight of steps that descend to the lower lawn terminating at the lily pond.*

bottom right: *Angel's trumpets,* Brugmansia sanguinea *has grown to nearly three metres tall in a sheltered corner.*

66

Set in rolling green pastures with cattle grazing right up to the gravel forecourt, 'Rosel Manor', home to the Lempriere family for over five generations is steeped in history.

A long drive, lined with blue mophead hydrangeas on one side and ancient parkland trees leads first to an old granite archway, the only remnant of the original manor house and a medieval colombier (dovecote). The Lempriere family can be traced back to 1367. The manor house that we know today was built in 1770 by Charles Lempriere, the Seigneur of the time and the Gothic-style turrets and cement coating (which had suddenly become very fashionable) were added some fifty years later.

From as early as the 15th century, Rosel Manor has extolled a fine garden. Writings show that Renaud Lempriere expected all guests to admire it. It now extends to about five acres with considerably more farmland.

A wrought iron gate opens onto steps that lead down to the Chapel Garden. The chapel itself is wrapped in wisteria and has a beautiful glass window, designed by Sir John Everett Millais who was a frequent visitor to the manor. Beside the chapel, the lawn slopes down to the first of two ponds. Records show that it was there before the reformation and is as old as the chapel and the colombier. It once guaranteed a plentiful supply of carp for the ancestral household.

STEEPED IN HISTORY

When the late Brigadier Raoul Lempriere-Robin and his wife Sheelagh arrived in 1964 many of the large camellias, magnolias and rhododendrons were already established. Camellias start flowering in the autumn with the old *C. sasanqua* varieties such as 'Narumi-gata' and continue until early summer. Under a protective canopy of trees, wonderfully varied in leaf, bark and blossom, naturalised snowdrops, wild narcissi and sheets of bluebells drift in between rhododendrons and the woodland edge, the brilliance of their hues contrasting delightfully with the fresh greens from emerging foliage.

facing page: *A restful view of the chapel and tranquil pond which used to supply the ancestral household with carp.*

Although there is plenty to enjoy all year round, the garden peaks in the spring when the colours are at their most intense. The exception is the summer border that runs downhill to the first pond and is backed by a high stone wall that is host to an *Abutilon megapotamicum* with conspicuous lantern-shaped flowers borne from summer into autumn. It is brimming with colourful geraniums, crinums, dahlias, sedums and asters that attract both bees and butterflies.

Across the lawn, dominating a corner of the Chapel Garden is a huge recumbent multi-stem *Magnolia* x *soulangeana* planted over a hundred years ago, it now has an impressive spread of over fifteen metres. A picture in April, when its chalice-shaped flowers open before the leaves unfurl, and again later, when the exquisite flowers of *Cyclamen hederifolium* sparkle at its feet.

Before progressing too far into the valley and not to be missed is the Palm Garden. Flourishing there are sasanqua camellias, winter's bark, *Drimys winteri,* tall chusan palms, *Trachycarpus fortunei* and in a sheltered corner a surprisingly large banana plant! Myriad pink and white daisy flowers, *Erigeron karvinskianus* seed into every crevice of the old stone walls.

The fish pond is fringed with moisture-loving primulas of the candelabra group and vast clumps of arum lilies. On the surrounding banks Kurume azaleas give a dazzling display and form an impenetrable carpet of colour, varying from crimson through to salmon, pink and white. An awesome sight at the edge of the pond is a *Taxodium distichum,* probably one of the

tallest in the British Isles reaching the great height of thirty metres or more. Another swamp cypress, not quite as tall, is to be found further down the valley. Continuing on past the second pond, with the chapel behind you, can be seen the turrets of Rosel Manor rising majestically.

A circular route is possible taking the path down the right hand side of the second pond, crossing over and returning on the other side back to the Chapel Garden. There are also a network of paths that traverse the hillside rising up to the manor house.

In the valley can be found a marvellous collection of rare and beautiful shrubs and trees; Australian tree ferns, *Dicksonia antarctica, Cornus kousa* from Japan and of exceptional beauty, *Magnolia campbellii* subsp. *mollicomata* 'Lanarth' and a large spreading *Parrotia persica* that is particularly noted for its late season colour. In autumn, the paths beneath the ancient oaks are littered with acorns and tiny cyclamen peep out above fallen leaves.

Towards the bottom of the valley, the vegetation reverts to native woodland; fallen tree trunks are left in-situ, moss and ferns envelop an old boundary wall, ivy shines amongst dead leaves and the stream runs down and into the sea as it has done for hundreds of years.

far left: *Ancient parkland trees at the entrance to the manor.*

top left: *Virginia creeper in its autumn coat dressing the front façade.*

bottom left: *View through an arch in the Palm Garden towards the chapel and manor. A flourishing banana can be seen on the left. Autumn in the Chapel Garden and valley is almost as delightful as in the spring. The whole garden turns into a magnificent glowing technicolor of oranges, yellows and scarlets.*

above: *A certain amount of control is needed to prevent vigorous creepers from smothering the chapel.*

top far right: *Reflections of autumn.*

far right: *Cyclamen hederifolium sparkle amongst fallen leaves.*

right: *The Palm Garden.*

71

A TOUCH OF THE EXOTIC

Inheriting 'Roselands' from his father in 1969, John Le Gallais and his wife Anne found themselves with a labour intensive Victorian garden of straight lines, box hedges and espaliered apple trees. In making the garden simpler and more manageable, they have introduced lawns, a concentration of shrubs and a splattering of perennials. "If you depend solely on trees and shrubs for colour and interest you will find there are periods in the year when the garden offers little excitement!" says John.

The garden has developed by degrees. Firm believers in having a solid framework, John and Anne, with a young family and a working farm, set about a skeleton planting that would survive the test of time. "If there is a framework of shrubby things and it goes through a period of neglect, the fabric will be there for when there is more time". Of course, many of the perimeter trees and shrubs of seventy years ago also remain to form a visual backdrop for new ideas.

Anne is the designer, responsible for the structure and shape, as can be seen by the clever positioning of New Zealand flax, that add a dynamic charge to the centre of the canvas.

On the south face of the house an existing Banksian rose is happily joined by a *Carpenteria californica,* a *Fremontodendron californicum* and a fragrant *Trachelospermum jasminoides* with a number of scented plants hugging their feet including *Daphne odora* 'Aureomarginata', lavender and chocolate cosmos. In front, a blue cedar, *Cedrus atlantica* Glauca Form is silhouetted against the sky and imposes a sense of scale. The planting reveals layers of historical and more recent planting with schemes focused on favourite genera.

Flagged steps are host to self-sown lady's mantle and lead down, between shrubs and the yellow bed, to an open sunny lawn. Borders flow around the perimeter, imaginatively filled

with the choicest of flowering shrubs, contrasting foliage and many rare treasures.

The Dell, a secluded sunken corner in which to sit, is almost hidden by the dense planting of shrubs such as *Hoheria sexstylosa,* which freely produces honey-scented white flowers, *Artemisia arborescens* 'Faith Raven' and a Judas tree, *Cercis siliquastrum.* Low growing plants cascade over the wall breaking any hard lines.

The design of the garden pivots around the classical beauty of the sundial which creates the central vista. A gift to John's father by the members of the Royal Jersey Agricultural Society on the occasion of his silver wedding. The quadrant beds surrounding it are anchored with a weeping pear and tiered *Viburnum plicatum* 'Mariesii'. A touch of originality and providing an exotic note are four *Phormium tenax* 'Rose Glow' which send up spears, bronze margined with pink.

The shape of the pergola echoes the elegantly proportioned beds

73

facing page: *A white gate divides the shelterbelt planting across the lane from the main garden.*

left: *A blue Atlas cedar,* Cedrus atlantica *Glauca Form planted close to the front of the house imposes a sense of scale.*

and provides an attractive sense of movement. In summer it is host to an exuberant display of roses in cream, buff-yellow and pink including the ramblers 'Emily Gray', 'The Garland' and 'Félicité et Perpétue'.

Beyond, gum trees including *Eucalyptus viminalis* are planted in grass and a white gate is festooned with *Rosa* 'Albéric Barbier'. Across the lane is a shelterbelt of poplars and alders planted after the 1987 storm.

Returning up towards the house, borders are crammed with colourful conifers such as *Thuja plicata* 'Zebrina' and *Chamaecyparis lawsoniana* 'Winston Churchill' and hollies, *Ilex aquifolium* 'Silver Milkmaid' and *Ilex aquifolium* 'Myrtifolia Aureomaculata'. *Robinia pseudoacacia* 'Frisia' and *Choisya ternata* 'Sundance' add splashes of gold and choice shrubs such as *Hoheria angustifolia* 'Borde Hill' and *Eucryphia* x *nymansensis* 'Nymansay' succeed in the shelter producing white flowers late in the summer.

Sumptuous borders line the drive and exemplify Anne's skill in planting. Among the tapestry of green, yellow and cream are a collection of pittosporums, many of which originate from New Zealand including *Pittosporum tenuifolium* 'Silver Queen' and *P.t.* 'James Stirling', both with leaves suffused with silver grey, 'Irene Paterson' with marbled green and cream leaves and 'Warnham Gold' with deep buttery yellow foliage, stunning in the winter. All conical in habit, *Pittosporum dallii* differs forming a large spreading shrub with leathery lance-shaped leaves and fragrant flowers in summer. Other outstandingly beautiful shrubs include the pyramid-shaped *Drimys winteri* and one of the best variegated shrubs, *Rhamnus alaternus* 'Argenteovariegata'.

The tennis court lawn is dominated by a large walnut, and a cider gum, *Eucalyptus gunnii*. *Pittosporum eugenioides* 'Variegatum' acts as a foil to *Fuchsia microphylla* which continues to produce tiny pendulous flowers right into the winter. John and Anne delight on Christmas Day, strolling around the garden, counting the number of blooms still to be found.

The most recent project, the Woodland, can be reached
either through the Anniversary Garden, which is home to
one of the loveliest maples, *Acer griseum,* or through a gate
flanked with pots of *Camellia* 'Spring Festival'.

Mainly planted in 1995, with the help of shelter planting
and rabbit protection, trees are now becoming established.
Hollies, including the less familiar *Ilex* x *altaclerensis*
'Camelliifolia' with beautiful camellia-like leaves and
eucryphias such as *E. lucida, E.* x *intermedia* 'Rostrevor' and
E. x *hillieri* 'Winton' provide a dark backdrop to fast
growing gums, Southern beech and wonderful birch such as
Betula maximowicziana and *Betula utilis* var. *jacquemontii*
'Silver Shadow', one of the most stunning with dazzlingly
white bark.

Perhaps most exciting of all is to discover superb members
of well-known families combining happily with tender
varieties carefully chosen by John and Anne.

above: *A sundial has become
the central vista to the garden
punctuated by four dynamic clumps
of New Zealand flax adding a
subtropical extravaganza.*

facing page top: *Urns
overflowing with petunias flank the
steps down to the lawn, sundial
and rose-clad pergola.*

facing page bottom: *A gate
is festooned with the semi-evergreen
rambler rose 'Albéric Barbier' which
has a wonderful show of creamy-
white flowers in summer.*

Hidden for eight months of the year is a garden and lavender plantation which from midsummer becomes immersed in a sea of purple and a flurry of activity for the Christie family.

From the end of May the air is filled with the scent of lavender, the senses are awakened and the sound of droning bees is all around. Orderly domes of aromatic foliage in shades of silver and palest green become tinged with ripples of mauve escalating into waves of velvety flower spikes.

It all began back in the early 1980's when David gave up his post as a schoolmaster in Shrewsbury to return to Jersey with his wife Elizabeth and their four children. An article, a chance meeting and a strange remark led to an introduction to Henry Head of 'Norfolk Lavender'. In the autumn of 1983 they took delivery of their first plants, all selected for their high yield of essential oils. Two other varieties have since been introduced, *Lavandula* 'Maillette' and *L.* x *intermedia* 'Grosso', known as 'Lavandin' in France and a stalwart of the

A SEA OF PURPLE

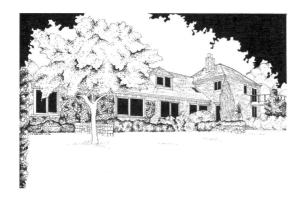

above: *Midsummer and the air is heady with the scent of lavender.*

French oil industry. 'Jersey Lavender' is now home to one of the National Collections of Lavenders. You can walk through the three main lavender fields which are planted with different varieties varying in tone, scent and flowering time. The harvest (or Lavandage as it has become known locally) starts at the end of June.

Close to the house is the herb garden, designed to be intentionally open, drawing you from one area to another without any obstacles or barriers. Paths form a series of intersecting diagonals and herbs are divided into their different uses, culinary, medicinal, cosmetic, dyeing and aromatic. In the centre of the unusual design is a dovecot and garden varieties of lavender such as *Lavandula* x *intermedia* 'Seal' and *L.* x *intermedia*

top left: *Vertical soldiers of x* cupressocyparis leylandii *'Castlewellan' contrast dramatically with a sea of lavender.*

top right: *All summer there is a constant humming of bees.*

right: *An interesting play on textures between the corrugated trunk and two wicker pigs.*

bottom: *Lavender fills the centre of the herb garden including* Lavandula *x* intermedia *'Alba'*

'Grappenhall' (a single plant can spread up to one and a half metres). Swathes of aromatic herbs entice you towards Sophie Ryder's delightful sculptures such as 'Lady Hare and the Dog' and where the paths cross, 'The Dancing Hares'. The air is an intoxicating mix of the heady scent of the flower spikes, the distinctive oils as they are extracted in the distillery and the smell of gum from surrounding eucalyptus trees.

Behind an ornate gypsy caravan (thought to be over one hundred and fifty years old) brought to the Island in 1920 by David's great-aunt, are the giant spires of *Echium pininana,* a silver wattle, *Acacia*

dealbata and a mountain gum, *Eucalyptus dalrympleana* with flaking patchwork bark. The sandy banks are planted as a pygmy pinetum and form a semi-formal transition from the herb garden to the woodland beyond and in a good summer lavender honey is produced from nearby beehives. The woodland, originally planted as a shelterbelt on sand dunes by David's grandfather was mainly Scots pine, *Pinus sylvestris*. Over one hundred and sixty were lost in the Great Storm of 1987. "It was quite oppressive really, but I never would have cut them down, so it was a blessing, it was all meant".

Inviting you to explore further is a simple *torii* gateway, painted red, the entrance to a collection of about seventy five different varieties of bamboos, one of the largest in private hands. Many originate from China

and Japan, some are rampant and need to be curbed, some are clump forming, all have different characteristics and amazingly, are thriving on sand. *Phyllostachys nigra* var. *henonis* with graceful canes wrapped in shiny green leaves and *Semiarundinaria fastuosa* which can make an excellent screen or tall hedge are just two species to be found.

A visit to the Christie's will linger in your memory not least because that most nostalgic of flowers with its powerful fragrance is the very essence of a perfect summer's day.

top: *Lady Hare, part of a partnership in the Herb Garden.*

above: *Where the paths cross, the hares dance.*

A GARDENER'S CHALLENGE

top: *A lovely combination - roses and iris.*

When I arrived Pat Jackson was sitting on the front steps shelling peas. Luncheon preparations were graciously forestalled to show me around her garden. An enthusiastic gardener, she spends many hours in her greenhouse propagating seeds and cuttings, most of which help to raise funds for the local gardening club of which she is secretary.

As an extension of the sand dunes 'Glenwhern', home to Pat and Philip Jackson, is in a marvellous position with access to the golf course and beach but gardening is only possible with the protection of massive windbreak structures. Plants must be adaptable to tolerate the sea spray together with soil that is free draining and as fine as talcum powder. Mulching with course organic material is essential and friends drop by with armfuls of clippings. Pat can often be found chopping pruning material directly onto the border where she 'treads it' in.

In the dry shade under giant firs, *Cupressus macrocarpa* are holly, *Pittosporum tenuifolium* and *Elaeagnus* x *ebbingei* with a dense cover of *Vinca major* 'Variegata', *Acanthus mollis,* sea kale, *Crambe maritima* and *Geranium macrorrhizum*. A windy corner is planted with a dark pink hydrangea backed by *Griselinia littoralis* and hostas (Pat has a regular slug hunt!) and house walls are hung with climbers including the vigorous *Clematis montana* and the lovely double white *C.* 'Duchess of Edinburgh'.

A Gold and Silver Border is backed by the most salt tolerant of the cypresses, *Cupressus macrocarpa* 'Goldcrest' and tough shrubs have been shaped into round drums including *Euonymus japonicus*

above: *Pink poppies self-sow around the garden.*

top right: Eschscholzia californica *intermingled with delicate grasses.*

middle right: Lavandula stoechas *'Marshwood'.*

bottom right: *A casual mix of lamb's tongue and swaying grasses.*

above: *Purple iris complement the golden foliage of* Robinia pseudoacacia *'Frisia'.*

'Aureus' and variegated privet. In front is *Libertia grandiflora, Iris* 'Pacific Coast' hybrids and sweet rocket, *Hesperis matronalis.* Variegated honesty and *Silybum marianum* self-sow contentedly and other interesting but unplanned arrivals are either potted up or given away. A purple fennel is allowed to stay!

An apple crusher is host to sun-worshippers – lots of grey foliage that require little water such as prostrate rosemary, blue rue and lavender. Old roses are chosen for their hardiness and hips, including tough varieties such as *Rosa moyesii,* burnet roses, *R. pimpinellifolia, R. p.* 'Williams' Double Yellow' and *R.* 'F. J. Grootendorst'. Procumbent roses such as 'Nazomi' and 'Partridge' scramble up supports and apple trees are underplanted with circles of flowers – alpine geraniums, rockery pinks and *Barbarea vulgaris* 'Variegata', in winter pierced by yellow and mauve crocus.

Among the plants that revel in the salt sea spray which blows on the garden are the stonecrops. Varying in character are *Sedum spectabile, S. telephium* subsp. 'Atropurpureum' and *S.* 'Autumn Joy'. Evergreens provide a backdrop to the red, purple and silver planting near the flag-pole and making brilliant patches of colour are red nasturtiums, gaillardias, *Geranium phaeum,* love-in-a-mist and catmint. *Lobelia tupa* produces magnificent red flower spikes each summer and an architectural red orach, *Atriplex hortensis* var. 'Rubra' is always a conversation stopper.

Further round, the border melts into buttery tones with cream *Eschscholzia californica* that are grown from selected seed, luminously delicate it makes a wonderfully impressionistic picture mingling with grasses, lamb's tongue and giant spurge, *Euphorbia characias* subsp. *wulfenii. Lavandula stoechas* 'Marshwood' add to the beguiling effect together with self-sown *Verbena bonariensis* around another apple crusher that is filled with aromatic thymes with charming names like 'Silver posie' and 'Lemon curd'. Shade is cast by two birch *Betula utilis* var. *jacquemontii* and an elegant snowy mespilus, *Amelanchier canadensis* which bears an incredible profusion of white flowers in May. A New Zealand flax makes a dramatic statement on the corner.

Near a greenhouse attached to the house, which in spring is bursting with seedlings, is the White Garden. There, are to be found hummocks of cistus, *Rosa* 'Iceberg', *Choisya* 'Aztec Pearl', geraniums and spreading mats of *Osteospermum* daisies. At the end of a winding path and deserving closer inspection is a *Solanum*

jasminoides 'Album' and nearby is a small pool overshadowed with more old roses, 'Zigeunerknabe' (Gypsy Boy) vigorous, prickly and covered in early violet-purple flowers and 'Variegata di Bologna'.

Pat Jackson has the voice of a true gardener, passionately observing every detail of every flower "I can see lots of things that I haven't planned - there are always surprises, sometimes its wonderful and other times not".

top left: Limnanthes douglasii *self-seeds freely and adds to the glorious colour.*

above: *Columbine, honesty,* Lunaria annua *'Variegata' and ferns in a shady corner.*

left: *Ixias spread in carefree abandon.*

AN INSPIRED CREATION

Occupied as a military headquarters during the German Occupation, when the late Lord and Lady Jersey arrived at 'Radier Manor' in 1947 there was no garden as such. Friends at the time said "You will never make a garden at Radier, nobody has ever made a garden there, so of course, that was the signal!"

In order to make a garden a shelterbelt was necessary and so young trees (oaks, limes and hornbeams) were planted on the two *côtils* either side of the valley. At that time there were views down the valley to the harbour. "You could have breakfast, see the ship coming in and get down (to the harbour) in time to pick up one's guests!" Now you can enjoy shady walks along mossy paths in the daffodil woods and come across unexpected vistas.

The Walled-In Garden is a delight with rows of flowers for cutting; hybrid tea and floribunda roses in perfect condition (and not a hint of blackspot), lily of the valley, gladioli and kaffir lilies. Bearded iris and lavender edge the paths and the air is filled with the magic perfume of *Trachelospermum jasminoides* hugging a high south facing wall. At the lower level is a collection of magnolias that have reached grand proportions, including *Magnolia sieboldii* with fragrant nodding flowers followed by eye-catching red fruit, *M. campbellii* and the evergreen *M. grandiflora*.

Outside the Walled-In Garden choice trees include a pocket handkerchief tree, *Davidia involucrata*, a *Eucryphia* x *nymansensis* 'Nymansay', *Styrax japonica* both in the white form and the pink *S. j.* 'Pink Chimes', originating from Japan. A fragrant cloud of

mock orange reaches up to five metres and a 'Kiftsgate' rose festoons a neighbouring tree.

The Water Garden is vivid with orange, yellow and pink candelabra primulas and moisture-lovers such as skunk cabbage, *Lysichiton camtschatcensis,* Solomon's seal and iris. Luxuriant ferns and hostas straddle the path, dragonflies dart amongst the waving wands of *Dierama pulcherrimum* and visiting kingfishers

facing page: *Two deer grace the edge of the lake.*

top left: *A beautiful jar adorns the perfect niche next to a yellow banksian rose.*

middle left: *The Walled-In Garden glimpsed through a peep-hole window.*

bottom right: *A vertical sundial overlooks the Walled-In Garden.*

can occasionally be seen. Well placed on a sloping bank, a *Garrya elliptica* tumbling and frothing wildly gives an unforgetable winter performance.

The late Lord Jersey had a fantastic eye, developed from his mother's rock garden in early childhood when friends teased that the labels were bigger than the plants! "I would say not such a large border, but in fact it was absolutely right in proportion" says Bianca, Lady Jersey. Large borders are filled with magnolias, rhododendrons, roses, such as the hybrid musk

'Felicia', paeonies such as *P. lactiflora* 'Cheddar cheese' and hostas. A show-stopper in March is a stunning *Stachyurus chinensis* that produces pendulous racemes of translucent yellow flowers. Banks in the Well Garden are planted with conifers, heathers and Japanese azaleas and the Hot Bed is home to a yellow flowered bottlebrush, *Callistemon salignus*, *Vestia foetida* and a glory bush, *Tibouchina urvilleana*. An imposing set of steps up to the house is flanked with huge round umbels of deep blue agapanthus flowers and the house walls are draped with a climbing pink geranium and the deliciously scented *Dregea sinensis*.

A wisteria-clad pergola offers some shade in the Swimming Pool Garden and the air is filled with the heady scent of roses and aromatic hummocks of rockery pinks and thyme, accompanied by neat domes of hebe, hypericum and magenta geraniums.

top: *View of the lake and surrounding parkland.*

middle: *Steps rise up to the manor house flanked by huge clumps of blue agapanthus.*

bottom: *A view to the lake.*

Inspired by a visit to Japan, the Camellia Walk was planted in 1967. The steep borders are massed with *C. japonicas* such as *C. j.* 'Pink Champagne', *C. j.* 'Lady Vansittart', *C. j.* 'Arajishii' and *C. j.* 'Magnoliiflora' in a decadent array of white, red and pink. A white wrought iron seat offers some respite at the top. Other camellias, planted as cuttings make a luxuriant show along the entrance and short drive.

An ornamental *Cornus controversa* 'Variegata' has reached perfection with horizontal, tiered branches covered in narrow creamy edged leaves. Nearby a resplendent horse chestnut towers above the area and a tulip tree, *Liriodendron tulipifera,* is a spectacle both in midsummer when it is covered in yellow-green tulip-shaped flowers and in the autumn when the leaves turn to a rich golden yellow.

A stroll along the poplar avenue (underplanted with hawthorn) is a joy for the view alone, the scale of the place can be seen across to the other side of the wooded valley with its winding paths and the pond below.

"The garden is alive and changing all the time, it requires patience but the reward is enormous." Lady Jersey is delightful and has a wonderful way of talking to her plants and in turn they all become her close friends.

above: *From the poplar avenue, views can be seen across the valley to the daffodil woods on the other side.*

To find this outstanding garden so close to the town centre of St Helier is an amazing discovery. Aptly named, 'Steephill' was, until recently, the home of Mrs Shepherd-Cross who has spent over forty years creating the magnificent gardens. Although planning was not done on paper there is a clearly defined structure, with terraced borders sloping steeply away from the house south-east to the valley below. A line of poplars help to buffer the ever-increasing noise from traffic and protect the ingress of urban development.

The house, designed by Ernest Newton, an English architect who specialised in 'the smaller country house' was built at the turn of the century in a neo-Georgian style with an imposing semi-circular portico.

Beyond a large lawn in front of the house is a wonderland of trees and shrubs. "Walking around 'Steephill' is like walking around the world" said Roy Lancaster on one of his many visits to the island. Plants from both hemispheres are represented in abundance although Mrs Shepherd-

A SANCTUARY ON THE EDGE OF TOWN

Cross insists that the garden started very casually and has evolved using whatever plants were available, planting one of this and one of that to cover the ground.

First take a look at the magical fernery beyond the conservatory. This wonderful cool grotto made of volcanic lava stone was once embellished with glittering ormer shells and is now home to a collection of ferns and cool temperate plants.

above: *Cherries have been trained into an umbrella shape, beyond can be seen the Chusan palms.*

facing page: *A gnarled black mulberry,* Morus nigra *in the valley.*

Back in the garden, a golden *Robinia pseudoacacia* 'Frisia' contrasts with a *Parrotia persica* and yellow crocosmia make a sumptuous combination, reflecting the egg yolk centres of a group of white poppies, *Romneya trichocalyx*.

Hidden behind an informal hedge of *Camellia japonica,* a small arched gate opens into the rose garden. Surrounding banks are contoured and tall Chusan palms, *Trachycarpus fortunei* add a distinctly subtropical atmosphere together with an ancient fan palm, *Chamaerops humilis* and a thicket of miscanthus. A high wall provides shelter for a *Solanum crispum* 'Glasnevin', *S. jasminoides* 'Album' and an architectural loquat, *Eriobotrya japonica*. There are two large greenhouses; in one is a tree echium, *Echium fastuosum* and the other (a vinery) is flanked by mounds of the delicate *Myrtus communis* subsp. *tarentina* and triumphs with a fruiting orange and grapefruit.

There are an enormous number of fine specimens in the garden such as an outstanding *Magnolia grandiflora* and an almost tropical *Podocarpus salignus* and from the white seat amongst the azaleas can be seen a striking *Drimys winteri*. The many levels provide a

sense of visual enjoyment and invite exploration and there are several paths that lead down the steep slope to the pond. Pause on the way to admire the view across the valley and the exotic plantings of maidenhair tree, *Gingko biloba* regarded by some as sacred, dawn redwood, yuccas and New Zealand flax.

In the Cutting Garden, a high granite wall offers protection to a host of mouth-watering climbers. All fragrant, a vigorous honeysuckle, *Lonicera japonica, Trachelospermum jasminoides* (which oozes a delicious sweet perfume) and *Mandevilla laxa* vie for attention. The Chilean jasmine is exquisite with scented white flowers and flourishes here, although normally treated as a conservatory plant. Winter sweet, *Chimonanthus praecox* extends the scent trail into the colder months.

Steps lead down to the valley floor; here you will find an ancient black mulberry, *Morus nigra* that is almost sculptural and wonderful examples of *Viburnum plicatum* 'Lanarth'. The pond and stream course are fringed with iris, bergenias and hostas; ostrich ferns, *Matteuccia Struthiopteris* sway above delicate primulas and astilbe grow beneath the vast leaves of a *Gunnera manicata*. Unusual trees such as the Kentucky coffee tree, *Gymnocladus dioica* and a pocket handkerchief tree, *Davidia involucrata* thrive, protected by a shelterbelt of poplars, limes and conifers planted in the middle of the last century and golden mimosa ignite the valley early in the year.

The mood induced by the garden is one of pleasure and highly fragrant calm, time escapes you and only the distant rumble of traffic returns your thoughts to civilisation and the outside world.

facing page top: Euphorbia griffithii *'Fireglow', iris and hostas fringe the pond and stream course.*

facing page bottom: Viburnum plicatum *'Lanarth' in the valley.*

left: *Forcing pots are both useful and decorative.*

below: *Nature's way.*

This property has now changed hands.

A DENDROLOGIST'S DREAM

It is a joy to arrive at 'Oaklands' on a cold winter's day and to breathe in the sweet fragrance of the christmas box, *Sarcococca confusa* that is planted either side of the front door. A resplendent silk tassel bush, *Garrya elliptica* 'James Roof' makes an ideal neighbour in the courtyard together with a burgeoning wisteria.

The Bonns began garden planning in earnest when they inherited 'Oaklands' in 1973. The house was built in 1811 as a working farm and priority was given to Elizabeth Wood and South Wood as essential windbreaks. Elizabeth and the late Michael Bonn (former chairman of the International Dendrology Society) have fulfilled their dream by planting a remarkable arboretum. In under thirty years 'Oaklands' has become a large rambling garden that invites a leisurely wander. The

above: *A frothy sea of lady's mantle washes over the terrace, lit by a golden* Cassia corymbosa.

left: *A ram's head evokes an image of contemplation.*

lawn stretches out to the south (which once was the bull field) and is interspersed with an island bed and curving borders. Now a frothy sea of lady's mantle washes over the terrace lit by the golden-yellow flowers of *Cassia corymbosa* and complemented by blue ceanothus. Beyond can be seen a border of 'Frensham' roses eventually to be superseded by a new planting of magnolias.

At the base of a wall just outside the Swimming Pool Garden is a colony of winter iris, *Iris unguicularis* which flower freely for several weeks and through a honeysuckle-clad arch is a floriferous *Camellia* x *williamsii* 'Donation', a cutting from the original plant at 'Borde Hill' in West Sussex raised this century by Colonel R. S. Clarke who was also a great tree man and where the Bonns used to live. Surrounding the pool is a hedge of golden leylandii that reaches about ten metres in height, a nightmare to cut, trimming is carried out once a year with the aid of tubular scaffolding.

In the borders around the south lawn there is a wonderful *Drimys winteri, Camellia* x *williamsii* 'Jury's Yellow' which is actually white but with a distinctive mass of creamy-yellow petaloids and most memorably, a *Magnolia campbellii* that normally waits at least twenty years before flowering! In August a large *Eucryphia* x *nymansensis* 'Nymansay' is a vision of white followed by another smaller flowering variety *E.* x *intermedia* and at the far end, the polished mahogany bark of *Prunus serrula* shines against a dark holly, next to a stunning *Cornus alternifolia* 'Argentea'.

94

top: *View from the terrace across the garden.*

second from top: *A statue awash with lady's mantle draws the eye towards the 'Frensham' roses beyond.*

middle: *Robust clumps of Crocosmia 'Lucifer' at the water's edge.*

bottom: *View across to the pond.*

A long bank of glossy red and pink camellias were planted along the old drive and *Pinus radiata* makes a dramatic silhouette against the southern sky. Beyond it lies a pond surrounded by notable trees such as *Nyssa sylvatica, N. sinensis* and *Magnolia* 'Iolanthe'. Fiery trusses of scorching azaleas animate the scene in spring and temporarily steal the limelight. Beside the water there are loosely dispersed groups of *Euphorbia griffithii* 'Fireglow', arum lilies, *Zantedeschia aethiopica* and *Z. a.* 'Green Goddess', iris and in early autumn there are flashes of scarlet from robust clumps of *Crocosmia* 'Lucifer'.

Rare and unusual trees all give promise to the arboretum which is now between fifteen and twenty years old. Fluid in its layout there are all sorts of discoveries to be made. In winter it is the striking *Acer* x *conspicuum* 'Phoenix' with its spectacular coral bark, but equally desirable is a rare heavy scented *Michelia doltsopa* 'Silver Cloud', the yellow flowered *Magnolia denudata* 'Elizabeth' and an epaulette tree, *Pterostyrax hispida*. In spring the woodland floor is coloured by emerging snowdrops, dainty cyclamen and clumps of daffodils.

On the other side of the house is the Kitchen Garden with a 'hedge' of globe artichokes and Michael's Folly, wonderful in May to stroll under the high arches, the perfect foil for a delicious tumble of wisteria and laburnum that leads to a hidden enclosure.

The Bonns have made a dream come true, a legacy for the future, a joy for visitors now and for generations to come.

right: *The winter stems of* Acer *x* conspicuum *'Phoenix'*.

IN
THE FRENCH STYLE

Approached by three long avenues, each with its own entrance lodge is a unique chateau set in magnificent grounds. The elegant manor house in part dating back to the sixteenth century is set in the midst of one hundred and thirty nine acres and has wonderful vistas overlooking parkland, ponds and pastureland.

Acquired from the late Major John Riley in 1995, Mrs Pamela Morgan has carried out extensive work to both the house and the gardens restoring the manor to its original glory. It had been home to the Riley family for three generations. Athelstan, John's grandfather who undertook the major transformation of the house in the early 1900's, doubling its size and adding the imposing French-style roof, would find the garden revived, not only planted with trees and shrubs that he would have known and cherished, but also with exciting newcomers creating in places a romantic and subtropical atmosphere.

above: *Palms add a subtropical atmosphere.*

facing page: *View over the canal to the lake.*

Partially cobbled, the centre of the courtyard is dominated by a circular water feature which was originally a French drinking trough and surrounding walls are draped with creepers and wall shrubs such as the early summer-flowering lobster claw, *Clianthus puniceus*, *Berberidopsis corallina* which has dangling crimson flowers in late summer, the fast growing *Eccremocarpus scaber* and a sumptuous *Abutilon* 'Nabob' with burgundy flowers that continue into autumn. Beneath them is a rich planting of smaller shrubs and perennials including *Cautleya spicata* 'Robusta', *Salvia bulleyana* and *Phygelius* x *rectus* with theatrical names such as 'Devil's Tears', 'Salmon Leap' and 'Winchester Fanfare'. Colours are warm apricot, soft orange and red, spiked with touches of blue.

Through an opening in the wall is the Chapel Garden. Narrow winding paths wrap around island beds of mixed planting, especially lovely in spring when a Judas tree, *Cercis siliquastrum* vies with a magnolia and Japanese azaleas are crowded by showy camellias,

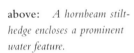

above: *A hornbeam stilt-hedge encloses a prominent water feature.*

right: *In scale with the manor is a monumental Lucombe oak,* Quercus x hispanica *'Lucombeana'.*

followed soon after by an unusual *Cornus capitata*. Other shrubs merge into each other creating the impression of an undulating sea of green. But beware the exquisitely beautiful but vicious spines of the Japanese bitter orange, *Poncirus trifoliata*.

As the setting demands structure, well-manicured hedges and the clipped box parterres provide formality to the south façade and visually contrast with the lake and open pastureland beyond. The beauty of the garden lies not only in the unforgettable imagery of grandeur and times past but also in its simplicity and clean lines.

Dominating the south lawn and perfectly in scale with the manor is a monumental Lucombe oak, *Quercus* x *hispanica* 'Lucombeana'. It is a cross between the deciduous Turkey oak, *Quercus cerris* and the evergreen cork oak, *Quercus suber* which is probably why it does not lose its leaves until very late followed almost immediately by fresh growth in early March. Known as the King's Oak, it is reputed to have already made a presence at the time of the visit of King Charles II during the Civil War when, exiled in Jersey, he sat at the heavy stone table which is still under it today. There are those that discount the theory as records show that the Lucombe oak first arrived in England in the mid 1700's although other romantics believe that the seed may have arrived long before, from Europe.

A stilt-hedge of hornbeam, *Carpinus betulus* frames the tranquil view to the lake and the Bosquet and encloses a formal, circular water feature. Either side of the wrought iron railings are tourelle staircases which lead down to a small canal and towards the tower is a lovely old cherry under which is a very accommodating semi-circular seat.

Concealed behind a yew hedge is the Swimming Pool Garden, where subtropical and tender species brush against old favourites. *Echium wildpretii* sway above the stately orange spikes of *Kniphofia caulescens* and *Fascicularia bicolor* contrasts with *Aeonium arboreum* 'Schwarzkopf' and creeping *Euphorbia myrsinites.*

Steps rise to the large walled garden in which a Mediterranean Garden designed by Tom Stuart-Smith revolves around a Gloriet of powerfully fragrant *Trachelospermum jasminoides* surrounded by hummocks of dwarf lavender, *Lavandula* 'Munstead'. Four olive trees, *Olea europaea* anchor the borders around the terrace and harmonise with other silvery foliage such as *Eryngium bourgatii, Stachys byzantina* 'Silver Carpet' and *Rosmarinus officinalis* 'Severn Sea' offset by flowers in soft purple, blue, apricot and pink. A scattering of cypress, *Cupressus sempervirens* and the tall plumes of *Calamagrostis* x *acutiflora* 'Overdam' give the garden a strong architectural character and add structure throughout the winter.

In the opposite corner is a Victorian Kitchen Garden with an impressive greenhouse that provides plentiful supplies of vegetables and next to it a tennis court will soon be hidden by the surrounding yew hedge. Through a wrought iron gate and across a gravel yard a new fruit garden is being made to maximise the use of high south and west facing walls.

The garden is perfectly balanced, there is a mix of formal and loose planting, serious and whimsical touches and that most elusive quality of scale, the proportions of different elements within the larger setting have been achieved in a disarmingly understated manner.

99

top: *Cypress,* Cupressus sempervirens *and* Calamagrostis x acutiflora *'Overdam' provide winter structure in the Mediterranean Garden.*

middle & bottom: *A whimsical touch.*

FROM VALLEY TO GARDEN ROOMS

left: *A large horse chestnut towers over the pond which is fringed by moisture-loving perennials.*

facing page: *Clipped in summer, a beech stilt-hedge will hold its leaves throughout the winter.*

'Grey Gables' not only encapsulates a lovely valley garden, but also a garden of rooms whether you visit in high summer or in the depths of winter when it is lit by a pageant of greens and a tracery of skeletal branches.

Celia Skinner has shaped the garden over the last twenty one years transforming a croquet lawn with square flower beds and no trees into a structured garden with a succession of changing views. Now there is a strong unifying factor that bonds together the individual areas. Sudden openings and vistas all help to catch the eye.

Perhaps the best way to approach the garden is to first stroll down to the valley. In winter take the mossy path, just left of the entrance gate. Here you will see a fine example of *Myrtus luma* with bark glowing like burning embers on a sunlit day. A leaning mimosa, *Acacia dealbata* is laden with swollen flower buds about to burst, an early rhododendron thrusts forth white flowers and camellias produce the first of several months of showy blooms. From spring onwards the colour is continuous. As the daffodils, violets and primroses fade, bluebells take over and smother the banks beneath rhododendrons, evergreen azaleas and magnolias.

Note the magnificent stand of black bamboo, *Phyllostachys nigra* which now reaches up to four metres in height and the heady fragrance of the winter honeysuckle, *Lonicera fragrantissima*. Steep steps lead down through alders and Himalayan birch, *Betula utilis* var. *jacquemontii*, to a series of leafy glades where magnolias, maples and bold groups of rhododendrons create an air of constant expectation. Colour is carefully orchestrated to create an harmonious symphony of purple, mauve, crimson, pink and white.

The vigorous *Rhododendron* 'Cynthia' with funnel-shaped crimson flowers, *R*. 'Sappho' whose flowers open white with a conspicuous blotch of deep purple and *R*. 'Polar Bear' produce a glorious

display and a succession of colour over a long period. Later lacecap hydrangeas add sparkle to their dark sombre leaves.

Finally the pond is in sight where hostas and skunk cabbage, *Lysichiton camtschatcensis* clamour for supremacy alongside primulas, iris, and daylilies. Other moisture-lovers include *Rodgersia aesculifolia, Darmera peltata* and *Kirengeshoma palmata* with creamy-yellow shuttlecock flowers, a bonus late in summer. Australian tree ferns, *Dicksonia antarctica,* seem to enjoy the damp margins and a wooden bridge crosses the water's edge to a small island dominated by an enormous horse chestnut.

Climbing back up, past mushroom-shaped Japanese maples, the steepness of the grassy hillside can be seen as you walk amongst the upper branches of walnuts and sweet chestnuts. Stop and you are sure to encounter a red squirrel high in the tree tops or to hear the rustle of hedgehogs nearby. If you are lucky you may come across the extremely fragrant and beautiful *Rhododendron* 'Fragrantissimum' and a carefully placed wooden seat.

Continue up as far as you can go and you will find the Holly Garden which partially hides a tennis court (although many of the hollies have succumbed to honey fungus and are being replaced). Stands of the variegated holly, *Ilex* x *altaclerensis* 'Golden King' provide wind protection for a young tender pine from the Canary Islands, *Pinus canariensis* which is slowly establishing itself.

Which route you take to the valley rather depends on the time of year that you are visiting. Certainly in spring you might follow the Camellia Walk, an avenue of laurels and camellias, mainly *C* x *williamsii* cultivars. Camellias include the popular 'Donation' with floriferous semi-double flowers, 'Glenn's Orbit', which is a seedling of 'Donation', and 'St Ewe' an upright form with rose-pink flowers. At the end of the Camellia Walk is a dramatic beech stilt-hedge equally effective as a screen both in summer and

winter. Part is underplanted with evergreen azaleas and heathers and part with clipped yew.

In front of the house is a flagged terrace and lawn with gently curving borders. On one side, sweeping conifers rise above a ground hugging tapestry of heathers and provide glorious foliage colour throughout the duller months, whilst on the other side, double herbaceous borders are designed to reach their peak from June until October and are filled with old fashioned favourites such as pink poppies, orange daylilies and white daisies. Although even in late autumn bright pink Guernsey lilies, *Nerine bowdenii* push through the thick mulch of well rotted horse manure and straw, followed by a witch hazel whose leafless branches are decorated with yellow spidery flowers.

The house, which was originally built by a painter named Le Maistre between the years of 1911-1914, is wrapped in wisteria and adjacent to the terrace is a rockery and small pool graced by the reclining sculpture of 'Circe' by Philip Jackson, and an Angel's fishing rod, *Dierama pendulum* that sways ethereally in the breeze.

In the little courtyard next to the swimming pool, trellis-clad walls are hung with powerfully fragrant *Trachelospermum asiaticum* and *Hardenbergia comptoniana*. Subtropical and half hardy plants revel in the warmth including *Acacia baileyana* 'Purpurea', a deep red abutilon, pineapple sage, *Salvia elegans* and *Anisodontea capensis*.

In contrast, a formal parterre is hidden within high hedges. Inside the neatly clipped *Buxus sempervirens* are summer flowering perennials. The centre may be filled with purple sage and *Geranium macrorrhizum* or lavender and the outer squares support *Anaphalis margaritacea* interplanted with pink campion and *Persicaria affinis* 'Donald Lowndes'.

In another enclosure a row of fastigiate hornbeam, *Carpinus betulus* 'Fastigiata' have recently been planted at one end and a granite wall offers protection for tender shrubs such as *Arbutus* 'Marina', *Azara microphylla* and *Hoheria sexstylosa*. On the opposite side, an escallonia hedge has been fashioned into a buttress design forming a series of niches in which to display small statues. At the far end is the pièce de resistance, a stunning latticework panel of firethorn, *(Pyracantha)* originally designed as a plaid of red, orange and yellow. Leading shoots are clipped twice a year to maintain the shape. Produced from cuttings taken from a single plant, *Geranium endressii* 'Wargrave Pink' not only serves as a dense ground cover but also clambers over a tree trunk that is draped with *Convolvulus sabatius* making an unusual 'table' decoration in the corner.

top: *Old fashioned favourites such as scabious and achillea rival for attention in the double herbaceous borders.*

bottom: *Delicate* Fritillaria meleagris *subvar.* alba *add seasonal charm to the rockery.*

The tiny White Garden is revealed only to the most inquisitive eyes. The design is simplicity itself, a white seat surrounded by billowing masses of white flowers. Fresh, pure and serene, it is the perfect place to relax, reflect and indulge the senses with the subtle fragrance of mock orange, *Philadelphus* 'Belle Etoile' and *Myrtus luma* 'Glanleam Gold'

right: *A latticework panel of firethorn.*

below *The formal parterre is hidden behind high hedges.*

Part of the Kitchen Garden is for herbs laid out geometrically around a central fountain. Beds are edged with variegated box and filled with amongst others, golden sage, marjoram, salad burnet and chives. Dwarf lavender and *Fremontodendron californicum* monopolise a sheltered wall border and *Vitis* 'Brant' scrambles urgently over iron

103

arches underplanted with misty catmint. Adding to this delicious mix are gooseberries, raspberries and currants whilst borage and lemon verbena grow near to a fig tree and sweetpeas clamber over intermittent obelisks.

This is a garden for all seasons, an inspired collaboration between man and nature. With endless energy Celia always has an eye to the next venture and the rewards that it may bring.

AN

ANCESTRAL
HOME

'St Ouen's Manor' has been in the de Carteret family since the twelfth century. It is now the home of Philip and Adèle Malet de Carteret and is surrounded by a moat and a stream that flows through the grounds and down to a wooded valley.

You know that you have arrived when you see the dramatic granite arch next to the Gatekeeper's Lodge. On the other side, an avenue of majestic trees beckons you in, as you gaze along the huge trunks of ash, beech and oak - the scale and restraint is awesome. Vertical lines are softened by the green verges and the perpetual play of shade patterns cast by the overhead canopy. This was once the main road from the town of St Helier to Plemont in the west until in the middle of the nineteenth century it was re-routed by Philip's great grandfather who was also responsible for much of the landscaping and the creation of the pond and stream course. If vehicles were banned you would surely be transported back in time!

The edge of the pond is broken by the overhanging branches of an enormous spreading ash, *Fraxinus excelsior* twenty five metres tall it must surely be a Champion tree in Jersey. Not only is this two hundred year old tree a remarkable legacy having survived intact, it is also host to a rare form of lichen which has created much excitement amongst the experts. Next to it is a huge beech which on close inspection reveals numerous dainty ferns and pennywort that have colonised around its bole. The sound of woodpeckers drilling can be heard regularly but they are rarely seen. Early in the year rhododendrons are prominent including

large clumps of *Rhododendron ponticum* backed by vast stands of bamboo. "I love rhododendrons and if you are clever you can have one in flower all year round !"

Near the pond is a magnificent purple beech that looks impressive in any season, whether in winter when its contorted limbs reach out across the lawn, or in spring as the pointed buds expand in sunshine, in full summer glory or as it turns colour in autumn. Other large beech add a timeless quality and maples lost in various storms have been replaced for posterity.

Surrounding the chapel are magnolias and camellias which bloom freely over a long period including a white flowered *C. sasanqua* which is smothered in bloom on Christmas Day and a nearby horse chestnut that spreads its canopy over an explosion of tiny orchids. Of the largest of the sweet chestnuts Philip says "Although they make such a mess I do get scared because it leaves very late in April. Each year I think it's dead and then it comes out and you can tell when it is midsummer's day because the leaves start to drop. Quite extraordinary. But it does bear a hundred pounds weight of beautiful chestnuts every year".

With your back to the colombier, the Walled Garden (for which Adèle has lots of ideas) and the three distinctive sweet chestnuts, *Castanea sativa*, you can see the manor buildings covered in Virginia creeper and anchored by surrounding trees. It is the calm atmosphere that makes it such a beautiful place with transitions of sun and dappled shade ensuring a rare combination of harmony and excitement. As with most architecture the manor as it is seen today has developed over hundreds of years, most of the building dating from the seventeenth century. Although there was a programme of modernisation in Victorian times it was not overly altered and much of its charm derives from the fact that it is a poetic evocation of passing time.

106

previous page: *Open swathes of grass and majestic trees create a stimulating patter of light and shade.*

top: *A magnificent beech near the pond, one of many that dominate the manor grounds.*

above: *Waterfowl take refuge in the pond whilst noisy peacocks strut through the garden.*

right: *Sunshine strikes
the manor in distinct
bright shafts.*

below: *Is it the mixture
of science and sentiment
that make sundials so
fascinating?*

Young Judas trees, *Cercis siliquastrum* have been planted on the mown grass in front of the manor and in time will make their presence felt particularly in late spring when their branches become wreathed in rosy-lilac flowers. Also of note is a *Magnolia liliiflora* 'Nigra', presented by the Men of the Trees which flowers profusely during late spring and summer, and a Brewer's weeping spruce, *Picea breweriana* makes a striking picture in front of the surrounding woodland which reverts to indigenous vegetation. Planted by Philip's mother, fifty years earlier, it is broadly conical in shape with sweeping branches. A thick carpet of ivy covers the woodland floor although in time Adèle would love to naturalise bluebells.

Moorhens huddle together and add intimacy along with a noisy peacock. Squirrels are not to be found in the grounds but are present inside the manor. As the family crest, they are embroidered onto cushions, hung in picture frames and decorate every available surface.

Sheltered from the prevailing winds is the sunny corner, baking in summer with the heat that radiates from the high granite walls. From here can be viewed the Lady's Walk, lake and wooded valley beyond. On the other side of the manor, seen over a fortified wall, is a small round fish pond and beyond is a field grazed by horses, once a medieval jousting field.

There is an overwhelming impression that it is the grounds that give cohesion and structural unity to the manor. It is a place that has survived the test of time, a veritable haven of peace interrupted only by the melodic sound of classical music floating on the air.

A HERBAL DELIGHT

A glimpse of still water and ripples from diving wildfowl, thickets of camellias and the rustle of tall trees swaying in the breeze and you have found 'Samarès Manor', home of Vincent and Gillian Obbard. The manor painted in soft cream is of gracious proportions and rests easily into the parkland setting surrounding it. Step back into a more elegant age as layers of Victorian, Edwardian and more recent planting are revealed.

From the avenue approaching the house (which dates in the main from the eighteenth century although parts such as the 'crypt' date back to the twelfth century) you will see the colombier or dovecot of Norman origin and the oldest in Jersey, a fine lime, tulip tree and a magnificent London plane, *Platanus* x *hispanica* that towers over the scene.

The inspiration for the gardens was due mainly to Sir James Knott in the early twentieth century who employed a landscape architect, Edward White to completely redesign the grounds creating the camellia plantation, the two large ponds, the Japanese garden with oriental summerhouse and within the walled garden, formal rose beds (which disappeared about fifty years ago). A staff of seventeen gardeners were employed and plants were acquired from all over the world.

108

facing page: *Little boy in the Herb Garden surrounded by a swathe of red valerian,* Centranthus ruber *and catmint.*

Hidden behind stone walls is a remarkable Herb Garden, designed in 1980 by John Brookes. While away the hours amongst the amorphous masses of red valerian, *Centranthus ruber* and the gently undulating spires of catmint, *Nepeta racemosa* 'Walker's Low' and walk around borders filled with sprawling herbs. Above all smell and touch the myriad scented ones.

Beds are designed in an abstract pattern balanced but not symmetrical and gravel paths separate rectangular blocks of planting. Near the steps is a small square knot garden edged in box and filled with alternately parsley and golden sage. The procumbent rose 'Oxfordshire' makes a charming centrepiece and surrounding borders are abundant, overflowing and full of old fashioned flowers and aromatic foliage. There are mats of velvety grey lamb's tongue, *Stachys lanata* 'Silver Carpet' and echoed diagonally across are delightful dark blue spikes of *Lavandula* 'Hidcote' punctuated by a giant clump of bear's breeches, *Acanthus mollis. Euryops pectinatus* continues to flower right into the winter, *Salvia microphylla* smells wonderfully of ripe pineapples and scented geraniums including *Pelargonium crispum* with crinkly lemon-scented leaves, dwarf *P.* x *fragrans* strongly smelling of nutmeg or pine and the peppermint geranium, *P. tomentosum* all merge together in muted shades.

Herbs are divided into their uses. Culinary herbs include salad burnet, lovage, angelica, creeping savory and sweet cisely as well as the more commonly grown parsley, chives and thyme. A large golden bay, *Laurus nobilis* 'Aurea' anchors the planting scheme. For pot-pourri and cosmetics there is orris root, *Iris* 'Florentina', elder and evening primrose and fragrant strewing herbs include *Rosa rugosa,* clove dianthus and lemon verbena and for ailments there are a host of remedies including St John's wort and garlic chives. Trained over iron arches are old apple varieties carefully pruned to shape by Vincent.

The Water Garden is built in limestone that was quarried in Cumberland and transported to Jersey, reputedly in two shiploads. Cordylines and *Trachycarpus fortunei* add to the subtropical feel together with other luxuriant marginal planting and sinuous paths cross over stone bridges and wind through the rocky outcrops. A wisteria, with gnarled and twisted branches reaches out across the lawn.

Stroll past a dawn redwood, *Metasequoia glyptostroboides,* the Japanese summerhouse and a glade of young willows and you will reach the Japanese Garden. A waterfall cascades over limestone boulders into another pond, originally built as a swimming pool (steps into the water still remain) and now full of koi carp. The edge is broken by leafy patches of iris and ferns, *Cotoneaster horizantalis* and evergreen azaleas. A striking swamp cypress, *Taxodium distichum* with knobbly 'knees' (above-ground growths from the roots) can be seen on the island.

Samarès is a garden that appeals to your emotions. As the air is filled with rich and varied aromas all the senses become aroused and all are satisfied. I can think of no better way of losing yourself for a few hours.

facing page: *Contrasting foliage -* Eucalyptus gunnii *and the autumn cloak of sumach.*

top: *A Japanese Buddha framed by the vivid autumn colour of* Parrotia persica.

bottom: *The air is filled with rich and varied aromas in the Herb Garden.*

First impressions are of giant firs, *Cupressus macrocarpa* reaching up to the sky, a sweeping drive, lush green lawns and an extraordinary house fringed with dark evergreens yet allowing an uncomplicated view to the sea.

Home of the inventor Ron Hickman and his wife Helen, the 'Villa Devereaux' was completed early in 1983. Existing trees, mostly towering pines and Monterey cypress, were retained as a buffer from the prevailing wind although many were damaged or lost in the Great Storm of 1987. Designed around an existing lime tree (recently felled) this unique house with its unusual buttresses sits comfortably into its setting.

The wonderful equilibrium of the space resides in the interplay of the contours, straight lines and languorous curves. On arrival, light plays an important part in the atmosphere as the sun rays filter through an overhead canopy casting long shadows over well manicured lawns. The combination of evergreens and deciduous trees such as alders and limes has achieved the desired effect. Birch make a striking composition followed by an old leaning pine, probably *Pinus sylvestris* creating an almost oriental picture over a ring of gold *Euonymus fortunei* 'Emerald 'n' Gold'. Next to it a sculpture by George Kowsan called 'The Green Green Grass of Home' dazzles in the overhead sun. Camellias form a dense mass against which can be seen their sumptuous blooms in red, pink and white including an old favourite *Camellia japonica* 'Adolphe Audusson' and *C.* x *williamsii* 'Jury's Yellow'.

In late spring the garden is particularly delightful as camellias are having their final fling, rhododendrons and azaleas take centre stage. The climax of the camellia display is usually early to the middle of March although it does vary from year to year. Nearby are magnolias including the evergreen *Magnolia grandiflora*, a flowering cherry and a sculpture called 'Torso' by John Skelton.

facing page: '*The Green Green Grass of Home*'

below: *A ring of gold on a winter's day.*

LUSH GREEN TO SEA BLUE

Borders are generous with burgeoning shrubs repeated in groups providing a strong sense of rhythmn juxtaposing *Elaeagnus* x *ebbingei*, *Viburnum tinus* and *Skimmia japonica*. Shapes contrast, architectural *Mahonia* x *media* 'Charity' and *Viburnum davidii* with turquoise-blue berries, weeping birch and vertical bamboo. There are winter performers such as *Garrya elliptica* with tantalising drooping catkins, witch hazel with flower clusters of sparkling copper, the skeleton framework of a weeping Japanese pagoda tree, *Sophora japonica* 'Pendula' and the lichen covered bark of *Prunus serrula*. But the *pièce de résistance* must be the stark tree sculpture that punctuates the skyline out of a dense cover of conifers and heathers, still standing after fifteen years. In summer, lively splashes of colour are added to the carpets of violets, *Pachysandra terminalis* and *Waldsteinia ternata* together with bold swathes of blue agapanthus.

In the shelter of the house is a Japanese style garden. Here the domed cut-leaved Japanese maple, *Acer palmatum* 'Dissectum' grows in ordered harmony

with bamboos, dwarf pines and prostrate conifers. There is a tranquility that derives from using plants sparingly with gravel and boulders. Colour is limited, low mounding evergreens and indigenous azaleas are used in small groups to offer peace and quiet contemplation. A corkscrew hazel is carefully pruned to appreciate the full beauty of its wiggly stems and the sacred bamboo, *Nandina*

below left: *Giant limbs explode into the sky*

below: *A shrouded figure*

domestica has found a special place (other invasive bamboo have been potted). There is an awareness of restraint and humility.

Helen, a First Grade Somu, practises the art of Ikebana and artistically shaped branches and curving stems are carefully chosen from the garden; perhaps an azalea twig covered in lichen; a pine branch or a piece of sacred bamboo, to this she might add just a sprig of Japanese quince or a single flower.

A large expanse of lawn stretches south with breathtaking views over St Brelade's Bay and dips towards the sea interrupted occasionally by a few rocky outcrops and a sculpture called 'The Embrace' by Geoffrey Thornton. The hypnotic sound of the sea is broken only by the sound of screeching gulls and the intermittent hammering of a distant woodpecker.

facing page top left: *In the shelter of the house is a Japanese style garden.*

top right: *A lantern marks the way through Japanese azaleas.*

bottom left: *Bamboo and stone form a simple water feature.*

bottom right: *Carved out of stone 'The Embrace' dominates the south lawn.*

The approach to 'Bras de Fer' is through a high granite arch. Immediately you are aware of a house
of distinction and charm and yet you can see little as all is hidden behind creeper-clad walls.
The present house dates from the nineteenth century and is the home of Diane and Jeremy Arnold.
A *Quercus rubra* in the centre of the gravel courtyard is surrounded by *Camellia sasanqua*,

A POOL OF GOLD

left: *Sentinel* Juniperus
communis *'Hibernica'*
juxtaposed with Libertia
grandiflora.

Arbutus x *andrachnoides* and other evergreens that soften the architecture and act as a foil for *Viburnum* x *burkwoodii* and *Parrotia persica* with its magnificent autumn cloak of burnished copper and red leaves.

A cornerstone Herb Garden edged in clipped box, *Buxus sempervirens* makes a decorative feature at the apex of two paths. One meanders down the valley, the other past shrub and floribunda roses that are grown as cut flowers including the soft apricot *Rosa* 'Buff Beauty', *R.* 'Iceberg' and *R.* 'Bonica'. In summer, they provide a glorious display edging the path to the old vegetable garden, now planted as an orchard with appealing varieties of apple including 'Bramleys', 'Russets' and 'Golden Delicious'.

Through a wrought iron gate into the main garden a high south facing wall is dressed with choice climbers, *Rhaphiolepis* x *delacourii*, *Carpenteria californica* with exquisite white flowers and *Actinidia kolomikta* with heart-shaped leaves marked cream or pink at the tip. In front, the herbaceous border overflows with *Acanthus spinosus*, *Agapanthus campanulatus*, kaffir lilies and *G. wallichianum* 'Buxton's Blue' and is studded with penstemons in different shades of pink.

A stunning evergreen *Magnolia delavayi* with exceptionally large paddle-shaped leaves flowers at the end of the summer and below is a mosaic of shade-loving plants such as *Persicaria campanulata*, hart's-tongue ferns and cyclamen. Around the corner are *Rubus henryi* var. *bambusarum*, *Sarcococca hookeriana* var. *digyna* and a cascading *Cotoneaster astrophoros*. *Choisya ternata* 'Sundance' hugs a granite seat accompanied by the creeping *Pachyphragma macrophyllum*.

In contrast the terrace has a Mediterranean feel. Sentinel *Juniperus communis* 'Hibernica' are juxtaposed with spiky *Libertia grandiflora*, creeping thyme weaves between cracks in the stepping stones and around a large oil jar is a dwarf hedge of *Teucrium chamaedrys*. Continuing the theme, sumptuous shrubs swell the west facing borders. Imposing bronze flax, *Phormium tenax* 'Purpureum' vies with a potent *Yucca* 'Vittorio Emanuele II' that pierces *Ballota pseudotictamnus* and the gamboge flowers of *Euphorbia characias* subsp. *wulfenii* loom above furry lamb's tongue, *Stachys byzantina* 'Silver Carpet'. This robust planting is then softened by the exquisite rambling rose, *Rosa* 'Albéric

top: *Symmetry and proportion in the formal garden.*

middle: *A mosaic of contrasting leaves.*

bottom: *In dappled shade Solomon's seal towers over hart's-tongue fern and hostas.*

117

Barbier' and above the wall can be seen the espaliered branches of a hornbeam stilt-hedge.

A pair of mop-head *Ligustrum lucidum* edged with box, flank the entrance to the formal garden which reflects the classical Georgian façade. Symmetry and proportion are the key. The south lawn is divided into four equal parts centred on a round reflecting pool with a small fountain and topiarised yews act as dramatic counterweights. The shape is echoed on the far side creating an intimate picture around a stone bird bath.

In dappled shade, snowdrops announce the arrival of another year followed in season by hellebores, Solomon's seal and ferns. *Hosta* 'Francee' and *H. sieboldiani* var. *elegans*, *Liriope muscari* and great swathes of *Crocosmia* x *crocosmiiflora* 'Solfaterre' are backed by old camellias and *Skimmia japonica*. A pair of *Corokia* x *virgata* 'Yellow Wonder' make curious talking points, laden with bright yellow fruits. In the sunnier beds a seat is softened by billowing masses of *Coronilla valentina* 'Citrina' with lemon-yellow flowers throughout the winter backed by a luxuriant vine, *Ampelopsis brevipedunculata* which after a hot summer is full of verdigris and blue fruits and a unique rose, *Rosa* 'Anemonoides' which bears a mass of pink single blooms. Here too are *Iris pallida* var. *dalmatica*, *Astrantia major* and the tiny *Alchemilla conjuncta*. In another bed *Cautleya spicata* 'Robusta' give a late burst of glorious colour. Steps rise to a decorative gate flanked by myrtles, beyond which is the tennis court and a narrow path to the pool.

The Swimming Pool Garden is stunning from early spring through to the end of summer. The bright azure pool gently encircles a bronze statue 'Nude Reading' by Sydney Harpley and a magnificent laburnum arch wraps around the water's edge. Beneath it are hummocks of *Potentilla fruticosa* var. *arbuscula*, *P. f.* 'Primrose Beauty' and *Genista dalmatica*, strappy yellow daylilies and

facing page top: *A focal point draws you along the Laburnum Walk.*

facing page: *'Nude Reading' surrounded by a pool of gold.*

top left: *An exuberant laburnum tunnel.*

top right: Rubus *'Benenden'*.

119

airy lady's mantle, mats of rock roses and creeping gold marjoram. In the gravel beds, the planting is distinctly more architectural. *Pittosporum tobira* with glossy green leaves and orange-scented flowers in summer, agapanthus, *Euphorbia schillingii* with lime green flowers and clumps of bergenia.

In contrast to the razzle dazzle colour around the pool, an amble down the winding path in the valley is calming. Trees and shrubs give way to grassy banks planted with spring flowering bulbs and at the bottom is a small pond, the marshy verges strung with wild iris and water forget-me-nots, *Myosotis scorpioides*; colours are muted and the green canopy is soothing. Here there are *Hoheria glabrata*, *Eucryphia cordifolia*, *Azara dentata*, *Rubus* 'Benenden' with gleaming white flowers at the end of spring and a lovely *Cornus controversa* 'Variegata'.

There are many sensations to be experienced from the brilliance of the Laburnum Walk in bloom to the soothing green in the valley.

A FLOWER FOR EACH DAY

Almost as far north as you can go is a country garden where you will find a flower in bloom every day of the year. Home of Lynne and Nigel Jenner, 'St Blaize' (the earliest part of the farmhouse was built in 1771) has a garden that is always on the move as new plant combinations are tried out and improvements are made. It is a garden that is and probably will never be quite finished! One of the biggest mistakes was in not planting trees at the outset to buffer the strong prevailing winds that whistle across the garden, which seventeen years ago was just a field.

Fragrant plants are particularly valued in winter; a sprig of wintersweet *Chimonanthus praecox* 'Luteus' or witch hazel, *Hamamelis* x *intermedia* 'Jelena' is delightful in the house and near the back door is a sublime *Dapne odora* 'Aureomarginata' and *Sarcococca confusa*. Colour, scale, contrasting shapes and texture (more and more grasses are finding their way into the borders) all play an important role and borders are themed to gently merge one into the other, perhaps with the odd 'shock' as a talking point!

Ilex aquifolium 'Bacciflava' backs the drive border with glistening golden berries and is a foil to the subtly scented *Camellia sasanqua* and summer hyacinths, *Galtonia candicans*. Beneath shrub roses, 'Golden Wings' and 'Windrush', are frothy lady's mantle, *Geranium* 'Johnson's Blue', daylilies, *Hemerocallis* 'Whichford' and *Aquilegia* 'Goldfinch'. An archway of cascading white and purple wisteria leads down to the pond underplanted with wonderful single paeonies in white and lemon, fringed with London pride and punctuated with box balls.

Low hedges of *Buxus sempervirens* 'Suffruticosa' define the internal boundaries of the cobbled Courtyard at the back of the house together with box spheres and mop-head acacias, *Robinia pseudoacacia* 'Umbraculifera'. Midsummer heralds the arrival of the old shrub roses, all highly scented including the exceptional *Rosa* 'Complicata', *R.* 'Charles de Mills' and the velvety dark red *R.* 'Tuscany Superb'. Scrambling through them are dark purple clematis *Clematis* 'Black Prince' and *C.* 'Petit Faucon' and at their feet are sweet rocket, *Hesperis matronalis*, *Galega* x *hartlandii* 'Alba', deep plum coloured alliums and dark penstemons such as *Penstemon* 'Purple Bedder', *P.* 'Garnet' and *P.* 'Osprey'.

Under the canopy of an early flowering cherry, *Prunus* 'Accolade' and *Acer negundo* var. *violaceum* is the Camellia Walk which begins with the sasanquas in October, *Camellia s.* 'Crimson King' and *C. s.* 'Rainbow' followed by a favourite *C.* x *williamsii* 'J. C. Williams', *C.* x *w.* 'St Ewe' and *C.* x *w.* 'Anticipation' joined by evergreen azaleas including 'Fedora' and 'Ho-o'. Romping around at ground level are trillums, lemon hellebores, *Smilacina stellata*, wood anemones, *Anemone nemorosa* 'Robinsoniana', *Narcissus* 'Hawera' and the unusual *Erythronium* 'Joanna'.

above: *A spring planting of* Erythronium *'Joanna',* Narcissus *'Hawera' and wood anemones.*

Under two ancient apple trees are bold swathes of snake's head-fritillary, *Crocus tommasinianus* 'Whitewell Purple' and the January flowering *Narcissus cyclamineus* and at the base of an *Acer griseum*, hellebores and the giant snowdrops *Galanthus* 'Magnet' put on a valiant display to beat the winter blues.

The Mound, one of the first areas to be planted has a wonderful combination of spreading white cherries, a snowball tree, *Viburnum opulus* 'Roseum', *Exochorda* x *macrantha* 'The Bride', the deliciously fragrant *Rhododendron luteum* and white *R.* 'Palestrina'. In this shady area bluebells multiply profusely spiked by *Iris sibirica* 'Perry's Blue', *Hemerocallis dumortieri* and shot with a little magenta from *Primula pulverulenta* along the stream course. Later in summer the colours mellow into pinks and mauve with *Astilbe chinensis* var. *pumila*, *Filipendula* 'Kahome' and the most discerning of grasses, *Hakonechloa macra* 'Alboaurea'.

The Azalea Walk, planted with Knap Hill and Mollis varieties, follows on with a crescendo of colour graduating from yellow through oranges to saturated red and then fading to warm pink and white. Great mats of blue gentians are visualised but alas - they struggle! Blue poppies are slowly increasing as are the tall *Cardiocrinum giganteum* but most precious is the Chatham Island forget-me-not, *Myosotidium hortensia* which is mulched every year with seaweed.

A multi-stem birch is reflected in the still water of the pond and flame coloured candelabra primulas colonise the edge together with a *Rheum palmatum* 'Atrosanguineum', *Podophyllum hexandrum* var. *chinense* and *Kirengeshoma palmata*.

A winter picture of *Prunus serrula*, birch and dogwoods such as the bright orange *Cornus sanguinea* 'Midwinter Fire' become masked in summer by a sea of blue agapanthus, including *Agapanthus* 'Blue Imp' and the tiny *A.* 'Lilliput' softened by unusual daylilies in subtle peachy tones, *Hemerocallis* 'Lullaby Baby' and *H.* 'My Belle'.

Island beds flow from yellow through to apricot, peach, pink,

123

blue and purple in subtle shifts of tone and hue. Grasses and perennials mingle in a carefree ensemble; *Salvia uliginosa* with *Verbena bonariensis*, *Aconitum* 'Bressingham Spire' with *Campanula lactiflora* 'Blue Cross', and *Salvia verticillata* 'Purple Rain' with *Kalimeris incisa* 'Blue Star'.

Clematis viticella 'Alba Luxurians' makes a tangled web with *Rosa* 'Phyllis Bide' and *R.* 'Gloire de Dijon' over a stone summerhouse that is encircled with flowers in white, flecked with apricot. Here can be found white agapanthus, *Verbascum chaixii* 'Album', *Aquilegia vulgaris* 'White Bonnets', spires of *Veronicastrum virginicum album* and globes of *Allium nigrum*.

124

Topiarised hollies, *Ilex* x *altaclerensis* 'Golden King', spectacular in spring when lit by vivid blue *Scilla siberica*, flank the archway through a bay hedge to the Swimming Pool Garden. Here there is a sense of place and memories of Provence. Large oil jars, an olive tree, hummocks of grey foliage pierced by silvery *Astelia chathamica* 'Silver Spear' and wands of *Stipa gigantea*. Flowers are blue, lemon and white; *Ceratostigma plumbaginoides*, *Kniphofia* 'Little Maid' and masses of highly scented 'Casa Blanca' lilies. There are jewels such as a Kangaroo Paw, *Anigozanthos flavidus* (brought back from the Great Ocean Road in Southern Australia), oleanders in lemon and white, the green candles of *Eucomis autumnalis* and the late flowering *Hedychium coronarium*.

top left: *Chatham Island forget-me-not,* Myosotidium hortensia.

left: Roscoea cautleyoides.

above: *Statue of 'Nicola' by Kate Denton (one of three in the garden) surrounded by a sea of blue agapanthus.*

A new addition to the south façade is a Victorian style
greenhouse and plans are underway to make a Rainbow
Garden, grading flowers in a dazzling array through the colour
spectrum, mixed with unusual edible leaves and vegetables. In
contrast a tiny Sunken Garden with a reflecting pool is a calm
oasis filled with luminous white flowers and surrounded by
the truly intoxicating scent of *Trachelospermum jasminoides* that
wafts across the garden.

A garden never stands still and much of the satisfaction comes
from the anticipation and planning of new schemes and plant
combinations.

above: *A tangled web of clematis.*

GARDENS OPEN TO THE PUBLIC ON A REGULAR BASIS

Samarès Manor
La Grande Route de St Clement
St Clement   (01534) 870551

Lavender Farm
La Rue du Pont Marquet
St Brelade   (01534) 746898

Judith Querée
Creux Baillot Cottage
Le Chemin des Garennes
St Ouen   (01534) 482191

Not included in the book, but well worth a visit.

Orchid Foundation
La Rue du Moulin du Ponterrin
Trinity   (01534) 861963

INFORMATION CAN BE OBTAINED FROM THE JERSEY TOURISM OFFICE AND GARDEN CENTRES.

Jersey Tourism Department and
Visitor Services Centre
Liberation Square, St Helier   (01534) 500700

Ransom's Garden Centre
La Grande Route de Faldouet, St Martin   (01534) 856699

Longueville Nurseries Garden Centre
New York Lane, St Saviour   (01534) 605006

St Peter's Garden Centre
L'Avenue de la Reine Elizabeth II, St Peter   (01534) 745903

Garden Scene Nursery
Douet du Rue, St Lawrence   (01534) 865779

Many of the gardens are also open on certain dates for charity, to groups by appointment and during Jersey Tourism sponsored events such as Wildflower Week and the Jersey Garden Festival.